Dear Reader,

Are you confused? Do you have any idea what is going on? Of course you are, and of course you don't.

This book is about bewilderment, a word which here means not having the faintest idea what is going on at any given time. It is also something of a murder mystery, in which a dreadful crime is investigated in the hopes of finding out what happened to the poor murdered victim. The person investigating is me. So is the poor murdered victim.

The clues in this investigation include a suspicious stranger, an upsetting supermarket, the strange way literature is made, painful embarrassment, long songs, improperly prepared eggs, and other things which I happen to think are important.

Some people might call *Poison for Breakfast* a book of philosophy, and hardly anyone likes a book of philosophy. When a person begins to investigate this bewildering world and their own inevitable death, they begin to suffer from a deeply troubling kind of bewilderment experienced by anyone foolish enough to love literature.

Unless you are that sort of person, I recommend reading something else entirely.

With all due respect,

Lemony Snicket

LEMONY SNICKET is the internationally bestselling author of the thirteen volumes in A Series of Unfortunate Events; several picture books, including *The Dark* and *The Bad Mood and the Stick*; and the books collectively titled All the Wrong Questions. His work has sold between seventy and eighty million copies worldwide.

MARGAUX KENT is an illustrator, thing maker, story gatherer, and wanderer. She co-founded Peg and Awl with her husband. They live in West Chester, Pennsylvania with their two boys, their dog, and a variety of other creatures.

POISON
FOR
BREAKFAST

Lemony Snicket

ILLUSTRATIONS BY MARGAUX KENT

ROCK THE BOAT

A Rock the Boat Book

First published in Great Britain, Ireland & Australia by Rock the Boat,
an imprint of Oneworld Publications, 2021

ISBN 978-0-86154-261-1 (hardback)
ISBN 978-0-86154-262-8 (ebook)

Printed and bound in Great Britain by Clays Ltd, Elcograf S.p.A.

Oneworld Publications
10 Bloomsbury Street
London WC1B 3SR
England

Stay up to date with the latest books,
special offers, and exclusive content from
Rock the Boat with our newsletter

Sign up on our website
oneworld-publications.com/rtb

In memory of the shoemaker.

POISON FOR
BREAKFAST

CHAPTER ONE

This morning I had poison for breakfast.

This book is about bewilderment, a word which here means "the feeling of being bewildered," and "bewildered" is a word which here means "you don't have any idea what is happening," and "you" is a word which doesn't just mean *you*. It means everyone. You have no idea what is happening, and nobody you know has any idea what is happening, and of course there are all the people you don't know, which is most of the people in the world, and they don't know what is happening either, and of course I don't know what is happening or I wouldn't have eaten poison for breakfast.

Everything that happens in this book is true, by which I mean that it all really happened, the poison and the poems, the deadly cactus and the hypnotic musician, the chicken and the egg and the fatal finale, a phrase which here means there is death at the end of the story. But the story begins at breakfast, which I fixed myself, as I enjoy doing. It won't be necessary for you to remember what I had for breakfast, because I will keep mentioning it, but it was

Tea
with honey,
a piece of toast
with cheese,
one sliced pear,
and an egg perfectly prepared,

and all of it, as I have mentioned, I fixed myself and ate all up while reading whatever I pleased.

I've been fixing my own breakfast for many years, beginning one summer when I was quite small, and I was with my family in a house we were borrowing. The house was on the shore of a lake which was quite large and quite cold, and a small flock of geese would gather on the sand, having loud conversations and making a mess. "The geese will go away," the owner of the house told us, "as long as you don't feed them," but the geese never went away, not all summer. In the morning, I would wake up and go by myself to the kitchen. The early sun would shine on the lake, the ripples so shiny and sharp that they looked like knives.

I read something once that describes the sea as "all a case of knives" and I have never forgotten it. It is a description I admire very much, because it is so startling that you know no one else has thought of it before the author did, and yet so perfectly clear that you wonder why you never thought of it yourself. All good writing is like this. It is why a favorite book feels like an old friend and a new acquaintance at the same time, and the reason a favorite author can be a familiar figure and a mysterious stranger all at once.

Although I had not yet read "all a case of knives" when I was living next to the lake, I would sit and watch all the sharp and shiny bits of water outside the window as I waited for the toaster to do its work. At the time, all I liked for breakfast was a glass of juice and a single piece of toast with jam on it, so I would pour my own juice and put two pieces of bread into the toaster. When they were ready, I would spread jam on one of the pieces, and go out to the lake and feed the geese the other one. They loved the toast and they stayed all summer and no one ever knew why. I kept feeding them for two reasons: A, because I liked feeding them, and it didn't seem fair to force the geese to look elsewhere for breakfast just because they were loud and had no bathroom of their own, and B, because I liked having a secret, and actually, as I write these two reasons, A and B, it seems to me that B is the more important one, and so B is actually A, the secret I liked having.

Sneaking out in the morning was such an interesting secret that I soon began to sneak out at night, which was even more interesting. The geese were gone by the time it was dark, and there was only the rustle of the water as I walked, the lake displaying its knives in the moonlight. Everything was quiet and noisy at the same time, and calm and spooky too. I was not yet writing books, not really, but I liked to stand in the darkness and think and write things down. Sometimes I wrote them down on paper and sometimes I just wrote them down in my mind.

I liked these times so much that I kept sneaking out at night when the summer was over and I was living in a house in a city. It is probably not necessary for me to describe the feeling of hurrying down a street at night, because you probably know how delicious it is already. It is, of course, also a little frightening, but feeling a little frightened is nothing compared to the dark blue sky and the one-eyed moon and the speedy chill of the night air through your pajamas. It is true that something terrible might happen to you walking around by yourself at night, which is why I always ran instead of walking, although this probably did not decrease my chances of something terrible happening. Something terrible can happen to you anytime— at breakfast, for instance.

As I ran I had an additional thrill, because at the time I liked very much a poem called "The Highway-man," in which the mysterious hero

came riding—
     Riding—riding—

just like that, with dashes between the words, making the poem more urgent and more fun to read. I would race around my neighborhood,

racing—

Racing—racing—

feeling as mysterious and heroic as the Highwayman, who incidentally ends up dead.

There's another line in the poem which rattled in my head as I ran: "The moon was a ghostly galleon tossed upon cloudy seas." A galleon is a type of old ship, but I didn't know that then, and because the word "galleon" looks like the word "gallon," I thought it was some sort of bottle, tossed on the sea with a message inside. I liked the idea that the moon had a message in it and that some night, if I kept racing around, I might be the person to receive it.

When I try to picture myself running around, I cannot see the neighborhood the way it really was, only the world of the Highwayman and a moon in the sky like a ghostly bottle. It is one of the mysteries of the world that you can change the landscape with your mind, that everything around you will move and shift just from the way you are imagining them. If your mind is on a book, for example, you may see the world of the book around you, even if you are not reading at the time. It is one of the many thrilling tricks of literature, but recently a shoemaker of my acquaintance reminded me that it can happen anytime, in any circumstances whatsoever. In fact, she spent some time when she was young walking a terrible landscape, without a book in sight, imagining only wonderful things. She, like the Highwayman, is dead now.

When I snuck out to do my nighttime running, I left through the back door of my house which led to a dark alley. One often hears the expression, "I wouldn't want to meet them in a dark alley," said about someone who looks or acts suspicious, but of course there is nobody whom you'd really want to meet in a dark alley. The alley I found myself in was like most alleys, full of shadows with eerie shapes and shifting sounds. I could have met my best friend in the world in this alley and they would have seemed like a menacing stranger. I felt like a stranger myself in this alley alone, a child believed to be in bed, but I would pause for a moment, before hurrying out to the sidewalk, to make sure I wasn't leaving anything behind.

When I was very young, someone told me the story of a kidnapping which had interested me very much. The kidnappers had grabbed a little girl from her bedroom and dragged her out into an alley where their car was waiting. The parents heard the noise of the car and hurried out to the alley, where the little girl's pillowcase was found. "Can you *imagine*," said the woman telling me the story, who was the sort of person who got gleefully excited when telling horrifying stories, "how *frantic* you would feel to find *your child's pillow-case* in a dark alley?" I could imagine this, so I always stopped to make sure I hadn't dropped anything in the alley that would make anyone frantic if they found it. I also sometimes kept watch by my bedroom window at night, looking for a kidnappers' car or any other sign of something terrible that might happen. A murderer, I thought, a werewolf. I do not know how to describe the way I felt when I was thinking about these things. I almost had to hold my breath, because it was wonderful and terrible at the very same time. Two hooded figures, a long snake, a pair of masked twins or a demon with a cloak. I would stand there, watching and thinking, for a long time, and though I never saw so much as a single witch, I continued to keep watch.

As you may have gathered, this is a different sort of book than others you might have read. It is different from other books I have written. There is a story to be found here—a true story about my eating poison for breakfast—but it is also a book of philosophy, a word which here means thinking about things and trying to figure them out. It is also a book about how I write the books I seem to have written, and some other things, like a long song and a movie I saw many years ago, which I happen to think are important. I've already told you that the book is about bewilderment, and about death, which has happened twice already so far, the Highwayman and the shoemaker of my acquaintance, and that it will end, as I've said, with a fatal finale.

All books of philosophy end up mentioning death, which is one of the reasons that many people do not like reading books of philosophy, just as many people do not like to leave their beds at night to sneak out of the house. I mentioned this book to another author I will not identify, and she said, "Oh, Mr. Snicket, who would want to read such a thing?" I know exactly what she means. If you enter a library looking for a particularly quiet place to read, head straight for the philosophy section. Because no one likes to read philosophy, no one will be there, and you will be undisturbed to read, to write or just to think and keep watch, as I do and have always done. It is part of being a writer—a very important part, even more important, perhaps, than writing things down. But it can be very difficult to describe.

When I was very young, for instance, after breakfast I would be told, "Please go brush your teeth and put your shoes on," and I would leave the room and then, at first very dimly and then much too loudly, I would hear my own name called, and would return to the breakfast room, my teeth unbrushed and my shoes off. "Mr. Snicket," I would be asked—I prefer it when people call me "Mr. Snicket," so that, eventually, if we become friends, I can say, "Oh, we've known each other for so long now, you don't have to call me 'Mr. Snicket,' "—"Mr. Snicket, what have you been doing?" and I would be unable to say.

At the breakfast table, back then, was a wooden chair that could be taken apart and put together in different ways. When you were a baby, it could be a high chair; when you were a small child, it could be adjusted to be a more suitable place to sit, and then again when you were an adult, and I always thought that perhaps it could be adjusted one more time when you died, to become a coffin—a "wooden overcoat," as I once heard it called—so you would only need one chair for your entire life. I'm fairly certain that when I am in my own wooden overcoat, I still won't be able to tell you exactly what I was doing when I had been told to brush my teeth and put on my shoes. I was not reading because I had no book in front of me. I was not writing because I did not have a pen or pencil in my hand. I was thinking. I was keeping watch. To try and explain it is bewildering, like having a startling message suddenly come to me, washing ashore in a bottle or perhaps slipped under my door, as it was this morning as I was finishing my breakfast and thinking of other things. It was just a scrap of paper, lying near the tiny sliver of nothing between the door and the floor. By the time I picked it up and read it, I could think of nothing else, for two reasons: A, because it was frightening, and B, because it was bewildering, and actually, as I write these two reasons, it seems B is the more important one, and so B is actually A, because it was bewildering. You can already guess what it said, as you read it at the very beginning of this book.

You had poison for breakfast.

Chapter Two

For a few moments I stared at the scrap of paper in my hands and tried to get my thoughts in order. I even tried to number them, in case it helped.

1. Egad!
2. There's no use thinking *egad*, Snicket. Remain calm.

No, wait, that should be your third thought.

3. Remain calm.

4. That's better.

5. Now, then, look at the message again.

6. *You had poison for breakfast.*

7. Egad!

8. Stop it.

9. Right.

10. Take a deep breath. It often helps to take a deep breath, or better yet, several deep breaths.

11.

12. That was just one breath. Take some more. Everybody knows how to breathe, but sometimes you have to stop and teach yourself once more how to do it.

13. *You had poison for breakfast.*

14. Stop! Take some deep breaths.

15.

16.

17.

18. All right, then. Now, do you think the note is some sort of joke? If you do, then relax. If you don't, skip down to 35.

19. Yes, a joke. It must be.

20. But what if it isn't a joke?

21. It certainly doesn't look like a joke.

22. A man is sitting on a train with a baby, who is very ugly.

23. In fact, the baby is so ugly that a nearby passenger says, "What a hideous baby."

24. "I've never been so insulted in my whole life," the man says, and hurries to the train conductor to complain.

25. "I'm so sorry, sir," the train conductor says, when the man tells her he was insulted so terribly. "I apologize on behalf of the railway company."

26. "Please allow me to move you to the first-class cabin, where you can enjoy a free glass of champagne,"

27. "and I will try to find some cheese for your pet rat."

28. That's an example of a joke.

29. It tells a little story and has a funny twist.

30. *You had poison for breakfast* does no such thing.

31. Of course, there's also the type of joke that is just a question with a funny answer.

32. Where does the king keep his armies?

33. Yes, that's a good one.

34. But *You had poison for breakfast* doesn't do that either.

35. All right, it's not a joke.

36. And if it's not a joke, then it's an emergency.

At the word *emergency*, I looked once more at the scrap of paper and agreed with myself. The words written there certainly felt like an emergency. Still, I didn't think contacting any emergency personnel—someone at a police station, for instance, or a hospital—was the thing to do. If someone had poisoned me, then I was murdered, and if someone hadn't, I wasn't, so contacting the police would be like calling the fire department and saying that either my house had burned completely to ashes or that it was still standing and I was just sitting around on the porch, and if I called anyone at the hospital they would surely ask what kind of poison it was and how much I had taken and how long ago I had taken it and would I please hurry over to be undressed and asked more questions and my only answers would be I don't know, and I don't know, and no, thank you.

I turned back and looked at my breakfast, although it wasn't really breakfast anymore. I'd finished every scrap of

Tea
with honey,
a piece of toast
with cheese,

one sliced pear,

and an egg perfectly prepared,

and all that was left was a damp cup and a plate with a few crumbs sitting next to the book I was reading. I always like to have a book with me at breakfast, although sometimes I do not read much of it. Some breakfasts I do not even open the book, but it sits beside me like a quiet companion while my thoughts wander all over the morning. I may be thinking of the day ahead of me, or the night I have left behind, or perhaps of things far from my own circumstances, until, in the blink of an eye or a sip of tea, my mind returns to the breakfast table, sometimes with a delicious new idea or a solution to some bewildering problem.

This is philosophy, more or less—the use of one's own thoughts to figure something out—and it occurred to me that philosophy might be the best way to solve the problem of my own poisoning. Not many people think of calling on a philosopher in an emergency, yet the most exciting and most useful things in the world have been born simply by someone thinking about them. Maybe it would work today, I thought. Maybe philosophy could save me.

At that very instant, for example, I was thinking about something: a story I'd read about some other people who had been bewildered at breakfast. The story is about a family called the Emersons, who lived in America, where their eldest daughter Sally was in love with a young man whom her parents didn't like. They much preferred a man named Stephen Jones, whose name stuck in my head from the moment I read it, because it made the man sound very dull. Sally apparently agreed, and made arrangements to sneak off and marry the man she liked better. But that very morning, the Emerson family was visited by an eccentric old woman who lived nearby. "Eccentric" is a word which here means "so unusual that people in the village thought the woman might be a witch," and she knocked on the door and asked for some breakfast. The family explained that they were very busy, but said that the old woman could come in and help herself.

This angered the eccentric woman, and she put a curse on the family, saying they wouldn't get any work done until sundown. Sure enough, after the old woman left, the Emersons found that their doors and windows were impossible to open, and that their cries to their neighbors were apparently going unheard. They were trapped inside their home, unable to attend to their work or their plans for romance. When the sun went down, the curse was lifted, but Sally had missed her appointment with her young man, who left town without her. I always remember the last sentence—"She married Stephen Jones, as her parents had hoped"—a bewildering ending to a bewildering story.

I read all this in a book which claims that the story is true—although of course you can't always believe what you read—but it is hard to say if it is more bewildering if the story actually happened or if someone made it up. Why would the woman, witch or not, be so angry at the family? "Come in and help yourself" is a remarkably generous response to a sudden request for breakfast, and the witch could have been enjoying

Tea
with honey,
a piece of toast
with cheese,
one sliced pear,
and an egg perfectly prepared,

in no time, but instead she put a curse on the Emersons. In most stories, witches put curses on people to teach them a lesson, but it seems unlikely to me that the family said, "Well, next time an old woman asks for breakfast, I suppose we'll drop everything and get cooking." Perhaps they even appreciated their time indoors, once they realized that they were truly stuck there, and enjoyed a quiet holiday from work, spending the day reading or teaming up to finish a jigsaw puzzle. Sally, of course, was probably not in the mood for such things, because her whole life had been ruined due to a missed appointment. But this is bewildering too. Sally's suitor, whatever his name was, seems a bit impulsive, a word which here means "too quick to leave town just because Sally didn't show up at a certain time." So perhaps it was for the best that she missed her appointment and did not marry a man who did not even write Sally a note saying, "Sorry to have missed you, how about we try again tomorrow at the same time?" Perhaps her life wasn't ruined at all. Perhaps Stephen Jones was not as dull as his name might suggest, and this was the beginning of a happy life for Sally Jones, née Emerson.

I stood looking at my breakfast dishes, clutching the scrap of paper and thinking of this story. "Née" is a French word which here means "born," although it is also often used to refer to a woman's first last name, in the event she changes it when she marries or flees from the law. This morning was née pleasant. Since breakfast it was fraught with danger. I looked at the words again, *you had poison for breakfast*, and although I knew, as you know, that you cannot believe everything you read, the ink on the paper seemed very believable to me. I had eaten poison for breakfast. Each moment I stood there staring at my scrap of paper was a moment closer to my death.

I did not want to die, of course. You are probably not looking forward to your own death either. It is likely that when you see death, real or imaginary, in the pages of a book or on a museum wall, projected on a screen or happening right in front of you, you think, *Well, I hope that doesn't happen to me.* But it will, of course. We are all going to die. You might die when you are very young (nobody wants that) so people will say that it's such a tragedy, you were so young when you died, or you might die when you are very old (supposedly, everybody wants this) so that they'll say that it's not such a tragedy because you were so old, or you might die somewhere in between, and people won't know whether it's a tragedy or not. You might die in a common accident, or in a remarkable one, remarkable enough that people who didn't know you still want to hear all about it. You might die of a disease (again, a common one or a remarkable one) which might be very sudden or quite protracted, a word which here means that it goes on for far too long. You might be killed by another person, either by accident, which is tragic, or on purpose, which is sinister, or by an animal, in which case figuring out whether it was tragic or sinister might be impossible. It might happen by surprise, or you might have plenty of warning, although no matter how much warning you have it probably won't seem like enough. It might happen late at night (burglary?) or the daytime (grease fire?), during a thunderstorm (puddle?) or a blizzard (toboggan?) or just a quiet breezy afternoon (old age, spoiled milk) in the middle of a celebration (trumpet, bad luck) or a swim meet (electrocution, jealousy), during a quiet evening at home (pneumonia, blanket) or a long drive in a tractor (revenge, cardboard box). Many, many more people have died than are living now, so when you die you will have something in common with the vast majority of human beings, but still it is as impossible to imagine as it is to avoid. You've probably tried to imagine it before, as I have, closing your eyes and lying still, the way you might imagine a food you've never eaten when you see it on a menu. But we do not know what it really tastes like.

It is easier to imagine our funerals. People will gather someplace, in a house of worship or at a cemetery or billiards parlor, and cry and carry on and offer their condolences, a fancy word for sad words that are only offered at funerals. Perhaps there will be a grand procession, which here means a kind of parade in celebration and grief. People might stand up and say kind things about us, and perhaps read out loud from books that seem meaningful or appropriate. Just last night I was reading a book containing passages which were read at funerals in ancient Egypt:

> You have journeyed over rivers of millions and hundreds of thousands of millions of years. You sail over them in peace and steer your way over the watery abyss, which is the place that you love.

I have very little idea what it means, but it sounds lovely, and it's nice to imagine people standing up and saying lovely things about me when I am gone, even if I might find the words bewildering if I weren't.

One nice part of thinking about a funeral is imagining people wishing they'd been kinder to us when we were alive. "Why oh why didn't I treat Lemony Snicket better?" I can almost hear them saying, over their very loud weeping, but of course some people will not feel badly at all when they learn I am dead. I'm sure you can think of people who, when informed of your death, will have trouble hiding small, nasty smiles. "Curse that person," they will say about you, like a witch who has been told she has to prepare her own breakfast, and they will think very hard about all your wicked ways. Most of these people are, naturally, wicked themselves, because you are probably very sweet and charming. But let's face facts. Some of these people will be right about you, because all of us have behaved badly toward other people whom we did not like for one reason or another. Sometimes I am in a foul mood and spend a few moments devising curses for people whom I do not like. I hope your hair falls out one afternoon at a restaurant, I think. I hope your teeth leave your mouth and run around town biting people and you are blamed and sent to jail. I hope you move to a new house and your new house smells horrible. I hope you step on a rug and it wriggles beneath you and you fall to the ground and bruise something. I hope the rug turns out to be a wolf that was sleeping on the floor and the wolf is angry and hungry and strong. To be fair, some of these people are wicked and so deserve to be cursed, I suppose. But then if we keep on being fair, some of these people are people I just happen not to like, and who would be shocked to learn that I occasionally imagine them being flattened by a falling chandelier.

It is one thing to think horrible thoughts, but it is another to behave atrociously, as you know. You can easily think of times when you were horrible, and when I say *easily* I mean it is very easy to remember these times and hard to stop remembering. They ache in the brain and the body, these shameful memories, like a broken bone that has never quite healed right. Once, many years ago, I was a young man in a hurry in the pouring rain, and I saw an empty taxicab which I ran to catch. I jumped into the back seat, grateful to be sheltered and on my way, when a man on the sidewalk grabbed my arm before I could shut the door, and I realized that the taxi had stopped for him, and not for me. "Please," he said, and gestured through the rain to a woman standing with him, who was pushing a baby carriage toward us. But I was already inside the nice warm taxi, and I shut the door. It was many years ago, but not a week goes by that I do not think about it, and wonder what on earth was going through my mind. I was in a hurry, yes, but it was not an emergency. I am certain that the little family did not perish in the rain, and that they found another taxicab, and perhaps have forgotten all about it, as it was so long ago. But I have not forgotten, and I would not blame them if they sat around occasionally, wishing that I would get my foot stuck between two heavy rocks as a swarm of furious hornets approached, or that every cracker I ever ate was stale. I get sad, when I think of my own wicked acts, although I suppose if I weren't sad about them it would mean I didn't care. I'm glad that I care, so I'm a little happy that I'm sad.

But in any case I will never see them again, that poor rainy family, so I will never get to apologize, which makes me sad all over again. When you apologize, it is a bit like reaching the last page of a book. The book is still there, with your wicked deed inside, but at least it is closed and put on a shelf. Every single thing I ought to have apologized for, and didn't, is like a book lying open and unfinished. When I do get to apologize, I like to say of my bad deed, "That was not my finest hour," and although "finest hour" is a phrase which means "a time when I was at my best," I like to think of my finest hour as an actual hour in which I am at my most true and good. I don't know when this hour is, whether it is in my future or if it went by unnoticed in my past, but I keep watch for those sixty shiny minutes. I know they are somewhere.

I stood thinking about all this, death and funerals and Egypt and taxis, holding the bewildering scrap of paper in my hands. I knew, of course, that one cannot go around looking for one's finest hour the way one can look for a lost glove or a deranged woman in a night-gown. But solving this poisonous mystery, I thought, investigating this message in my hands and perhaps even delaying my own death, would be something to do in my finest hour, if it happened to be now, and with that thought I went to the door and opened it, to see if there was any trace of whoever had slipped the message into my house.

If I were making up a story, I would have it gray and miserable outside, but it was sunny and miserable instead, glaringly bright and bitterly cold, as if the sky could not decide if it was in a good mood or would spend all day growling. I didn't mind this kind of weather, weather that cannot make up its mind, because I am often the same way, or at least I think I am. I don't know.

My home was at the top of a large hill, and a curvy road led down to the busier neighborhoods of the city, where I did my shopping and met my companions and visited my library and performed the other tasks that made up my daily life. I saw a man on the curvy road walking away from me. I could not see his face, and his clothes were rather ordinary, but I did not think he was someone I knew. He was no friend of mine, nor was he an enemy I recognized, someone who spends their time cursing me and wishing me harm. He was a stranger. I decided at once to follow him.

I grabbed my coat from a hook by the door. Slid-

ing my arms into the coat always reminds me of the
same thing—

Where does the king keep his armies?
Up his sleevies.

—but the scrap of paper I was pocketing was no joke.
I looked back at the ghosts of my breakfast—

Tea
with honey,
a piece of toast
with cheese,
one sliced pear,
and an egg perfectly prepared,

—and numbered my thoughts again, to get them
in order.

1. Don't think about your dirty dishes as ghosts,

I told myself.

2. Or how the chair looks lonely without you
   in it, Snicket—a wooden outline of someone
   sitting.

3. Grab a pen and a few scraps of paper, so you can take notes on your investigation.

4. In fact, perhaps you've already taken a note or two, while you were thinking about all those other things.

5. And bring the book you were reading at breakfast.

6. Remember what you learned, years ago: You're never sorry you brought a book.

7. Besides, it's a small book. Look, it fits easily in the pocket of your coat.

8. It's why you like that coat so much, because books fit in its pockets,

9. So you can take books with you on all your journeys.

10. Leave now.

11. Don't think about journeys,

but I couldn't help remembering a time when I sat in a room with several other writers, discussing how we made books, all the different stories we admired and the ones we disliked and the ones we wanted to write. One writer there was quite famous and very unpleasant, and he gave us all a disgusted look as we talked about all the different stories. There were, he said contemptuously—a word which here means "in a tone that indicated he found us as tiresome as we found him"—only two stories, really:

A stranger comes to town.

and

Someone goes on a journey.

The writer I liked best in the room, a woman quick with a joke and generous with kind words, murmured a secret to me: "Those are the same story." I asked her what she meant, and as I hurried out of my house to follow the unfamiliar man, I thought of her explanation, and wrote it down: When a stranger comes to town, they have arrived from someplace else, so someone has gone on a journey. She was right, they were the same story, and we laughed quietly together, while the famous and contemptuous author kept lecturing the room.

12. You have always been grateful to her, for lifting the curse of boredom on that long-ago day.
13. She's dead now.

CHAPTER THREE

I left my house as quickly as I could, pausing only to lock the door behind me. This took longer than usual because my hands were trembling a little. It occurred to me that trembling hands could be an early effect of being poisoned, and I wondered if soon my whole body would be trembling, or if my limbs would begin to ache or if my hair would fall out or if something ghastly might happen to my eyes and lips. To calm myself down I remembered that the trembling was likely just the result of excitement and nervousness and mystery and dread and suspense. Those are a lot of things to feel at once, and I was so busy feeling them that when someone spoke it startled me enough that I made several involuntary noises, a phrase which here means "sounds without meaning to." Involuntary noises are my least favorite kind of noise I can make. If I'm going to sound foolish I would at least like to have done it on purpose.

"Good morning," is all the voice said, and I turned and saw my next-door neighbor, sitting on her porch with a book in her hands. It was, of course, not a good morning for me, not so far. But I did not want to tell my neighbor about what was on my mind. She was not a neighbor I know well, certainly not well enough to share with her my troubling message. So I just replied, "Good morning," two words which always give me the impression that things are all right. If I find myself among strangers, at a bus stop for example, or in an elevator or a small island surrounded by crocodiles, and everyone says "good morning," then I know we are all civilized people and things will turn out all right. We will fashion a drawbridge from palm fronds and cross safely to the opposite shore, or repair the elevator cables using dental floss one of us happens to have with us, or the bus will show up on time. If I am the only one to say "good morning" and everyone else just looks at

the ground and mutters, then I know that the bus will
catch fire and everyone will be pushing others aside to
leap out the windows, or the elevator will have terrible
music playing but everyone will be afraid to say so, or I
will be singled out as chum, a word which here means
"person being eaten while everyone else escapes," so I
immediately returned my neighbor's greeting.

"Good morning," I said.

"What are you up to, Lemony?"

As I've mentioned, I don't enjoy being called by
my first name unless I ask someone to do so. Even
when I was very young, I preferred to be called "Mr.
Snicket" or even "Master Snicket," a term some people
use for young boys which has the additional advantage
of making the person saying it sound like a servant.

"I have some things I need to take care of," I told her.

"Errands?"

"In a manner of speaking," I said, using one of my
favorite ways of saying "No, you are wrong."

"When you opened the door you were looking all
over the place," she said. "I thought perhaps you had
lost something. Did you lose something?"

"My life, perhaps," I wanted to say, but instead I
just told her I hoped not.

"Somebody loses something," she said thoughtfully. "I remember someone told me that all stories could be summarized as *somebody loses something.*"

"I heard that it was either *someone goes on a journey* or *a stranger comes to town.*"

"But those are the same story," my neighbor said. "If a stranger comes to town, it means someone has gone on a journey."

My eyes were on the man walking down the hill. "Speaking of which," I said, "did you notice any strangers around recently? Someone on my doorstep, for instance."

"I'm not sure," my neighbor said. "To tell the truth I've been lost in my book."

"What are you reading?" I couldn't help asking her. Even in my hurry I was curious, as I always am, to see what book is in someone's hands, and when she showed me the book I felt as if it were a magnet and I were a paper clip tumbling toward it. "I love that book very much," I said.

"Do you?" she said. "I'm liking it so far."

"You've never read it before?"

"No," she said.

"I envy you," I told her as I walked away, and it was true. It's the sort of book that's so terrific you are almost sorry when you first finish it, because you will never get to read it for the first time again. I had a tingly memory of the first time I had read it, when a librarian of my acquaintance had slipped it into my hands. There are some librarians so trustworthy and so interesting that you know any book they recommend will be worth your time, and I didn't even wait until I had walked home to start the book she had given me. I was standing at a corner waiting for the light to turn green, when I opened the book to read it for the first time.

The book is about a family—a father with four children, who, years after his wife (the children's mother) dies, marries a woman with one daughter. The eldest of the four children is David, the hero of the story, and the daughter, David's new stepsister, is a rather mysterious girl who is interested in the occult, which is a word for witchcraft and ghosts and other things that make books more interesting. Soon the family home is haunted by a poltergeist, a word which here means "either a noisy ghost or a stepsister playing tricks," and David tries to discover which it is. It is challenging and sometimes frightening for David to solve this mystery, but he feels it is his responsibility to do so. He is the type of person, an admirable type, who wants to sort things out, and make the world as clear as he can possibly make it. "All of David's clues, and instincts," reads a part of the book I like very much, "seemed to indicate that he should be prepared for almost everything, and he thought he was; he hoped he was."

Sometimes in the book it seems like the poltergeist is one thing, and sometimes it seems like another, and creepy things keep happening at night which are scary even if you are reading them on a sunny day as you walk home from the library. It's an exciting book but also a thoughtful one, because the story manages to be about the difficulties of living in a haunted house and the difficulties of living with new people, and as I walked down the street, I thought of my neighbor on her porch, reading it for the first time, even though I could no longer see my neighbor, any more than I could see myself as a child, standing on the street corner and reading it for the first time myself, so it was as if two unseen people were with me as I walked. You could call them ghosts, but of course that was sort of a trick, to call them that, and I suppose this was something the book wanted you to think about—if thinking about people, being haunted by them, is the same thing as being haunted by a ghost. I thought about my neighbor, who could be thinking about the same things as she read the book, and how the author of the book would probably be pleased to know that two readers were thinking about precisely what she wanted us to think about, so that even though the author is dead her work still haunts people, which could mean she was a ghost too. And I kept on thinking about people who are gone from the world, walking down the street, just as I had walked down the street thinking about such things as I read the book for the first time, and I rounded a corner and saw that the man I had decided to follow, the stranger and perhaps even the person who had poisoned me, was gone.

He had vanished, although I don't know if "vanished" is really the word. He had just gone some other way—rounded a corner or walked into a building—I couldn't see. I couldn't see anyone else on the street either, not a single person, but that didn't mean everyone in the world had vanished. It just meant I happened not to know where they were. So this man had not vanished, either, but I did not know where he was, and I did not know what to do. It was bewildering.

I stood on the sidewalk and rested my head against a sign telling me to *Stop*. I took my pen out of my pocket and wrote the words "the stranger vanished" on a scrap of paper, but that didn't make me feel any better. I felt quite lost. I wasn't lost, of course—I was just a few blocks from my home—but I *felt* lost, the way I felt that the man had vanished even though he was just someplace I couldn't see, so I had to stand still and blink for a moment as I thought of what to do next.

As it happens, standing still and blinking is a perfect illustration of a certain principle of philosophy. It's a paradox, thought up by Zeno. Zeno was an ancient Greek philosopher who ended up being tortured by people who didn't like his ideas. Nowadays philosophers are hardly ever tortured, because most people ignore them completely, and it's hard to say which is the worse fate for philosophy and the people who practice it, being tortured or being ignored.

In any case, a paradox is something that is possible and impossible at the same time, and this particular paradox states that we cannot move from one place to another until we first move halfway there, which makes sense. For instance, if you are in a park, standing at a lamppost, and you want to walk to a bench, as in the illustration below:

you must first walk halfway there, which the illustrator is marking with an apple because she is hungry:

But of course, in order to get to the apple, you must also walk halfway there:

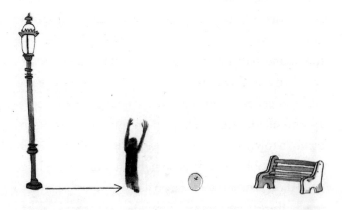

which the illustrator has marked with a mysterious shadow because she is not only hungry but suspicious. And of course, in order to walk to the mysterious shadow, you must first walk halfway there:

marked with a handkerchief because the illustrator also has a cold, and you can keep dividing this distance in half, never getting anywhere until you get halfway there, and halfway halfway there, and halfway halfway halfway there, and this is the paradox: Nobody can ever get anywhere, and yet of course people move around all the time. They go on journeys. Strangers come to town. If you look up from this book right now, you'll probably see or hear somebody going someplace, even though first they must go halfway there, and halfway halfway there, and it's bewildering to think about.

I stood there blinking and thinking for a moment, and then I decided to make a new plan. The stranger had vanished, whoever he was and whatever that meant, so my plan to follow him was of no use. But I still had the message in my pocket, just a little crumpled, and the poison in my body from my breakfast:

Tea
with honey,
a piece of toast
with cheese,
one sliced pear,
and an egg perfectly prepared,

and I lined up these items in my head as if they were suspects in a murder mystery. And perhaps they were, I thought. If I'd eaten poison for breakfast, then the poison must have been in one of these items, all of which were purchased in my neighborhood. I decided to visit the locations where each breakfast item—

Tea
with honey,
a piece of toast
with cheese,

one sliced pear,

and an egg perfectly prepared,

—had arrived into my life. One of these would be the scene of the crime.

I headed quickly down the street, happy to have a new plan but otherwise feeling sad, because I liked my breakfast very much, all of it, and I'm sure you can imagine what it feels like to suspect that an item in your usual breakfast was plotting against you, no matter what your usual breakfast might be. Different people eat different breakfasts, and have different ways of thinking about food. The shoemaker of my acquaintance, for instance, liked to take me out to dinner when I was a child. My family had taught me to eat everything on my plate, especially at a restaurant, where food is more expensive, and so whenever the shoemaker took me out I dutifully ate every bite. But the shoemaker had a different way of thinking. She thought that if you were providing someone with dinner, the only way to tell if they were satisfied was if there was food left on their plate, because it meant you knew for sure they were no longer hungry. So when I ate everything on my plate, she would summon the waiter and order another dish, as was her tradition, and as was my tradition, I would eat every bite, and then she would order something else, and I would keep eating and she would keep ordering and it was like another paradox, in which I was still hungry (according to her) and very full (according to me) at the same time.

When the shoemaker was old and dying, I sat by her bedside and reminded her of this, and she smiled. She was very weak then, and hardly spoke anymore, although I do remember one sentence she managed to utter, just days before she died. Another acquaintance of the shoemaker's had brought a dog to her bedside to cheer her up. The dog was friendly, and the shoemaker had always liked dogs, but she was not in the mood for a dog that day. Perhaps she was too busy dying, which is, from the look of it, very exhausting work. The visitor picked up the dog and put her on the shoemaker's bed, and the shoemaker frowned and struggled for a minute with her weakening mind and mouth, until finally she could say what was on her mind.

"Bye bye doggie," is what she said.

I murmured it to myself now, with the message in my pocket and the new plan in my head, heading down the curvy road toward the shops where I had bought the items for my breakfast. All my clues, and instincts, seemed to indicate that I should be prepared for almost everything, and I thought I was. I hoped I was. I did not want to stand around, blinking and poisoned. I wanted to leave my bewildering paradox behind. *Bye bye doggie.* It was time to go someplace, even if I first had to get halfway there, and halfway halfway there, and halfway halfway halfway there, before I arrived.

Chapter Four

The tea shop was my first stop, because it took just a minute to walk there, or even less if I was hurrying, and I was. It was a little curious to be hurrying to the tea shop, because drinking tea is usually the opposite of hurrying. Tea is difficult to drink quickly, because it is hot and needs time to steep, and so a cup of tea forces you to slow down and think as you wait for it to cool and become more flavorful. I was hurrying to get somewhere where I usually slowed down.

It was a familiar feeling, to be hurrying someplace without really knowing what is going on. When I was a child, this happened all the time, because when you are a child, nothing is your business, and you are constantly being yanked one place or another with no satisfying explanation provided by the adults doing the yanking, and so you soon get used to being in a constant state of bewilderment. You are yanked awake in the morning, often before you want to get out of bed, and you are yanked toward breakfast and away from the table before you are done. You are probably yanked toward school, whether or not you are in the mood, and it might be a school in which you are yanked from one room to another to learn about different things, or one in which you stay in one room and your brain is yanked from subject to subject no matter what you might be thinking about. Sometimes you have a good time and sometimes you do not, but never is there a satisfying answer if you ask *Why can't I stay in bed a little longer and read the poem about the sea being "all a case of knives"?* or *Couldn't I please instead just eat a little more toast and finish this chapter?* or *What reason could there possibly be that I must face the blackboard instead of looking out the window at the rain making quick tiny circles everywhere on the ground?* and even now, when I am an adult and sometimes find myself being asked questions like these, as my hand reaches out to yank someone someplace, I have no good answer.

When I was a child, I saw a movie on a screen in my living room which made me feel much better about never knowing what was happening. The heroine of the movie is a young woman named Eve, who arrives in a rainy city wearing a glamorous evening gown but without anything else whatsoever, including any money in her empty purse. This is confusing.

She hails a taxi, and asks the taxi driver if he will drive her around town all night without being paid, while she looks for a job as a nightclub singer. He agrees, and usually when a woman in a movie wants to be a nightclub singer, she manages to do so. In this case, however, she's a terrible singer, which is confusing.

The taxi driver is sympathetic, and offers to let Eve stay overnight in his apartment. Eve likes him, but is not interested in a sleepover, so she jumps out of his cab into the rainy night. She is still wearing her glamorous evening gown, so she manages to find shelter by sneaking into a fancy party to which she has not been invited, introducing herself as a baroness, a word for a sort of royalty which Eve most certainly is not. Some guests at the party invite her to gamble with them, and she agrees, hoping she will win some money, and because Eve has failed so many times in the movie so far, you might think that she will manage to win at gambling, but she loses instead, which is confusing, although more realistic.

Now Eve has to give money, which she does not have, to these party guests who are calling her a baroness, which she is not, but when she opens her purse there is plenty of money inside. This is confusing, and she is confused, but she gives the money to the guests, including a young man who insists on taking her from the party to wherever it is a baroness might be staying. Eve, of course, has nowhere to stay, but she names a fancy hotel, the sort a baroness might choose, and he takes her to the hotel, and when the young man takes her there, she is greeted by name— not her own name, Eve, but the name of a baroness, which is confusing—and she is given the key to an enormous and beautiful room, the sort where a baroness might stay.

This is so confusing that she goes to sleep, and in the morning, there is a knock on the door, and this was the most confusing of all, because at this point some adults came into the room and asked me what in the world I was watching and yanked me away to go someplace I can't remember for some reason I don't know. This made me feel better, because I didn't know what was happening, and neither did the heroine of this movie, but she seemed to be having a good time and I was having a good time watching her adventures.

From then on, when I was yanked someplace, I thought that perhaps I would be mistaken for a baroness and have an exciting adventure. Since then I've had many adventures, as you may know from other books of mine, although I've never been mistaken for a baroness, and I thought, as I approached the tea shop, that if I'd really been poisoned, then being mistaken for a baroness is something that might never happen to me, because there was no longer time to do anything but find out what had happened with my breakfast. The movie actually contains a warning to that effect, a warning that makes Eve nervous, a warning that even the most exciting adventures come to an end, often badly or sadly.

My tea shop was called Incomparable Tea, a name that has always confused me. The word "incomparable" simply means that you can't compare it to anything, and even though it is supposed to be a compliment—a way of saying something is so good that you can't think of anything else like it—it sounds more like a lie. Many compliments sound like lies, of course. Nothing will make you look for a mirror and a comb quicker than hearing "Your hair looks nice." But the word "incomparable" particularly makes me suspicious, because I am a writer, and comparing things to other things is part of my occupation. Over the years I've learned to compare almost anything to almost anything else. I can compare the pencil I am using to write these words (and these words, and these and these) to my own life, because it is sometimes sharp and sometimes dull, and because it is getting shorter and shorter the more I use it, and because even when I try to erase things you can still see the marks they left behind. I can compare my mother to an apple, because she spent some of her early days in a tree, and because I would like her less if she were baked and sprinkled with cinnamon. I can compare sadness to an automobile, because they can both run me over, and I can compare happiness to an aardvark, because they're both unusual to see early in the morning, and I can compare the various teas for sale at Incomparable Tea to all sorts of things, which means they're not really incomparable. There's a tea that tastes like freshly cut grass, and a tea that has a scent like campfire smoke. There is a tea that, when brewing in hot water, opens up like a flower, and one that dissolves into little threads like a lousy sweater. There are teas the color of a dying fern and an angry tree and a thrilling storm and dung.

The closer I got to the tea shop the more excited I became. I have always admired any store that sells only one thing, because it promises delight, the way a person who spends eight years learning how to make cake will probably make you a good cake, but a person who spends eight years as an aviator and a tailor and a math tutor and a trainer of bears in the circus will probably kill you in a plane he is flying very badly while wearing a shirt that doesn't fit and fighting off an ill-behaved bear, all the while insisting that seven times six is harmonica. I was eager to see all of the different kinds of tea, snug in jars and boxes and tins lined up on brightly painted shelves. I looked forward to sitting at one of the shop's little wooden tables, which always remind me of square lily pads on an inviting pond, and to wait for the teapot to start steaming like a friendly volcano. The tea shop is run by a man who talks too much and his daughter, who hardly talks at all, so you can direct all tea-related questions to the tea merchant of your choice, depending on whether or not you are in the mood for conversation. Any minute now, I thought to myself, I would arrive at the doors of Incomparable Tea, which are made from shiny glass with brass handles cool to the touch. There are words painted on each door in very pleasing type:

INCOMPARABLE TEAS FROM

on one door, and

AROUND THE WORLD

on the other, and it is particularly pleasing when a person is walking through one of the doors, so the message becomes

INCOMPARABLE TEAS FROM

an old woman, or two bald men

AROUND THE WORLD.

In mere seconds, I thought, I would walk through those doors myself,

INCOMPARABLE TEAS FROM

Lemony Snicket, and I was certain this admirable shop would help me with my investigation. Such a tea shop, I thought, might even have an antidote to whatever poison I had consumed, some steamy remedy to rescue me from death.

But when I arrived at the shop, a wooden sign had been put up on the door, so it read

CLOSED

AROUND THE WORLD.

Once, years ago, I was standing in an airport, when I heard a fluttering around me and I turned to see a small bird. It was a small brown type of bird, perhaps a sparrow, and it seemed quite frightened to be surrounded by building instead of sky. Who knows how it had gotten into the airport—an open window, perhaps, or through a door meant for airplane passengers—but now it was stuck. It was flying around a building built to help people fly, and it could not find a way to fly out to all the sky out there waiting. I often wonder what happened to that sad little bird, and I will never know. I hope it found another window, or another door, and I hope it is having an airy adventure someplace. Perhaps it has been mistaken for a baroness. But it seems more likely to me that it was stuck for good. There are times when one feels stuck in life, no matter how many wonderful shops are around or how much sky is nearby. The world can be wide open around you, but you can feel

CLOSED

AROUND THE WORLD.

Or, as I heard in a movie I saw a long time ago, "Every Cinderella has a midnight." You probably know who Cinderella is, of course—an ordinary person, like Eve, who is suddenly transformed into well-dressed royalty. It only lasts until midnight, and then Cinderella is stuck again, cleaning up after her stepsisters, her adventure over, at least for the time being.

I stood at the Closed shop and looked around, bewildered once more, wondering if my adventure was over so quickly. I wasn't much of a detective, at least the sort who'd be the hero of a mystery story. In most such stories, the person investigating the crime would be led closer and closer to the solution to the mystery. The detective might follow a person in the streets, and be led to an intriguing location where many secrets could be discovered. I have had such experiences myself, as perhaps you have read. But this is a different sort of book, describing a different sort of day. I had tried to follow someone, but they had vanished, and now my first intriguing location was Closed, with its secrets locked up inside. This was not like a mystery story at all. It was like—what was it like? My mind scurried for words but none of them sounded like good ways to describe how I felt, until I knew at last what I meant.

It was incomparable.

CHAPTER FIVE

I stood at the Closed door of the Closed tea shop for another minute or so. I had always admired Incomparable Tea's daringly erratic hours, a phrase which here means that no one knew when the shop would be open. It was unusual to run a shop this way, and a little brave too. It had made me even more hopeful that the tea merchants would be unusual and brave enough to help me, but now I was just standing at the locked door feeling displaced, a word which here means "as if

I were in the wrong location." Everyone feels this way sometimes, and some people feel this way all the time.

"Native," on the other hand, refers to something or someone closely associated with a certain place, such as the native birds that were chirping around me. The birds didn't seem to care that the tea shop was closed or that I was poisoned, and were flitting around having their own conversations in various branches and bushes which lined the sidewalk. There were several different kinds of birds, all familiar to me from the neighborhood, although I didn't know the names of them. It has never interested me much to learn the names of different birds, because, of course, you are not really learning their names at all, just names we call them. When a person tells you their name, they are telling you what they want to be called, but a goose or a sparrow, for instance, would likely be confused if they learned we were calling them these things. "Red-breasted robin?" a red-breasted robin might repeat in astonishment. "That's not my name. And why are you focusing on my breast? That's inappropriate."

The birds near the tea shop seemed to be speaking to each other, and I wondered if different kinds of birds speak different languages or if it just sounds like they do, or if "language" was even the right word for the sounds I was hearing. Some people call it "singing," as if birds are putting on a musical show, rather than talking to each other, and this seems a rather self-centered view, a phrase which here means "the selfish way we humans often think about animals." Many humans, for instance, believe in reincarnation, which is the idea that when you die you are reborn as a new person or another animal, and many of the people who believe in reincarnation believe that a human is the highest form, the best thing to be when you are reborn. I have never been convinced of this. I looked at the birds. They did not seem to be thinking I was the highest form, nor has any other creature I've ever looked at, and their chirping did not appear to be for my entertainment.

Some of the birds were of a type that I saw once just outside a building where I was hiding. There was a large patch of dirt, where some grass had died, and some of these birds were sitting in the dirt and wiggling, fluttering their wings in order to dirty themselves up. I had never seen this before and I thought the birds might be in some sort of trouble. Perhaps they were ill, I imagined, or injured somehow. Even though I do not know anything about birds, not even their names, I thought a human like myself could be of assistance, so I called an organization that helps animals native to the area where I was hiding, and described what I was seeing to the expert who answered. In reply, she uttered a sentence I have never forgotten.

"Yes," she said, and I could tell she was nodding. "They do that."

They do that. It was a simple and elegant answer to my question, and I realized the tea shop, even though it was

CLOSED
AROUND THE WORLD

had helped me with my investigation just as simply. While walking to Incomparable Tea, I had thought about how helpful the shop would probably be with my poisonous predicament, which made me realize now that there was nothing at all suspicious about them. I would move on to see the beekeeper who provided me with the honey I used for my usual breakfast. She worked nearby, as did her bees—they were both native to the area—and I had known her for years, so I did not suspect her of being a poisoner, but perhaps she had noticed something amiss, a word which here means "wrong about the honey she had sold me." I knew she was careful and observant. The jars of honey she sold all had carefully lettered labels reading *A Syrup of the Bees*, which was the name of her business and also a

book I have read. The author of *A Syrup of the Bees*
is F. W. Bain, although "author" is not quite the right
word. There are many books with F. W. Bain's name
on the cover, all with interesting titles—*A Syrup of
the Bees*, *A Digit of the Moon*, *Bubbles of the Foam*,
Essence of the Dusk—and all translated, by F. W. Bain,
from old manuscripts originally written by unknown
authors in Sanskrit, a language used in India. F. W.
Bain adds notes and explanations to his translations,
which I found helpful when I read *A Syrup of the Bees*,
which, if you are not used to old Sanskrit manuscripts,
is a very strange book, and a good book to think about
while walking toward a beekeeper.

The story concerns a king named Mahidhara, who
is also a sort of sorcerer, and he has one hundred
daughters who are sorcerers too. Mahidhara decides
that his daughters ought to marry, so he has a sort of
party, lasting one hundred days, with guests from all
over the kingdom so that each day, in order of birth,
one daughter will choose someone to wed. For ninety-
nine days, all goes well, but then the youngest daughter refuses to participate in this matchmaking party.
Her name is Makarandiká, a name which F. W. Bain
tells us means "one made of the honey or syrup of
flowers." Mahidhara and Makarandiká argue, and the
daughter uses her sorcery to change into a sea-bird, so

she can fly around for a little while and calm down, something I often wish I could do during an argument.

Some distance away is another king named Arunodaya, and Makarandiká swoops down to listen to him as he leans against a parapet, which is a fancy word for a balcony, and talks to a friend. Arunodaya believes in reincarnation, and in his last life, he believes, he was also a human being, and that he was married to a wonderful woman, and he would like to find that woman, who has also been reincarnated, again. The trouble is, Arunodaya explains on the parapet, he doesn't really remember his previous life, including this wonderful woman, so he's not sure how to find her. The only thing he really remembers is that she was from a well-educated family, or, as F. W. Bain explains it is said in the original Sanskrit, "of the pandit class."

Makarandiká has heard all this, and for some reason has decided that she is in love with Arunodaya. Still a sea-bird, she speaks to him, saying she is a messenger from the gods, and that the woman he is looking for will appear on a certain night at a ruined temple not far away. He eagerly agrees to go there, and of course Makarandiká shows up at the temple and presents herself as the reincarnation of his wife, a woman from the pandit class, which she is not. They marry, and everything works out well for a few years, until Makarandiká says the wrong thing.

The book, as I have said, was strange to me, and I had been grateful to F. W. Bain for his various notes and explanations which had made the Sanskrit story less bewildering as I read it then and thought about it now. The word *pandit*, for instance, would have confused me if F. W. Bain had not explained it to me, because before *A Syrup of the Bees* I had only seen that word as part of the name of a man whom I also found confusing. His name was Korla Pandit, and he was a musician who would appear from time to time on a screen in my living room. As I neared the corner where the beekeeper usually sold her honey, I thought of the invisible narrator, whose calm and quiet voice would introduce the musician as a man of the Hindu religion, from the Indian city of New Delhi, and a believer in the universal language of music. Then Korla Pandit would appear in a large, jeweled turban and, without speaking a word, he would play the organ. The music he played sounded strange to me, and it was strange that Korla Pandit never spoke or that nothing else much happened. Sometimes someone danced behind him, or there was a painted background depicting a desert landscape or the inside of a palace, but mostly

Korla Pandit would just play the organ without saying a word and I would just watch and listen. Music is often described as the universal language, a phrase which here means that everybody can understand it, although as with birds, "language" may not be the right word, and who knows if anybody, let alone everybody, can really understand music. I would stare at Korla Pandit on the screen, thinking about this silent man from India, but who knows if I was really understanding what it was he was trying to say?

It was not until I was an adult that I thought to do some research on Korla Pandit, who was dead by then, and what I discovered was much more bewildering than what I had seen on the screen. Korla Pandit was not Korla Pandit, and he was not from India. His real name was John Redd, and he was born in America. He impersonated an Indian man, though not very accurately—Hindus do not usually wear turbans, and the music he played was no more Indian than he was. His trickery didn't catch much attention, because he lived in America, and most of the people around him at the time knew very little about India or the people who lived there. A silent man in a turban apparently seemed believable enough. I imagine he must have felt displaced, spending his whole life in a fraudulent costume. John Redd was descended from people who were brought to America by force and sold as slaves. Slavery was more or less brought to an end in America, although not as quickly or apologetically as it should have been, and even after slavery ended, the descendants of slaves have been treated very terribly by many people in many places with much hatred and violence, which, like slavery, may someday come to an end, although also not as quickly or apologetically as any decent person would like. The descendants of slaves, in John Redd's time, were hardly allowed to appear onscreen in America, even if you were very good at playing the organ. It was easier and safer for John Redd to pretend to be from India.

I paused in the walk to sigh, remembering how sad and confusing this had been for me to learn. I, like many people, had assumed that Korla Pandit was who the calm and quiet narrator told me he was, and now I knew no more about him than the people around him knew about India. Shortly after this research, I walked by a bookshop and saw a book in the window called *Everything You Know about Indians Is Wrong*, and as I had been very wrong about what I knew about Korla Pandit, it seemed like something I should read. I went inside and purchased it immediately, and eagerly opened the book as I walked down the street from the shop toward a small restaurant, where I ordered a sandwich for lunch and kept reading. I remember that the sandwich was brought to me with fancy little toothpicks stuck into it, to help keep the sandwich from falling apart, and I was so fascinated with the book that I almost swallowed one of the toothpicks.

The book, however, is not about people from India, as I had assumed. I was wrong about *Everything You Know about Indians Is Wrong*, because it is about people native to America, who were called Indians by people native to Europe, who arrived in America believing it was somewhere else. The Europeans are sometimes described as "discovering America," which is confusing, because of course there were already people living there, so it would be as if I walked into your house and said I discovered it, simply because I hadn't been there before. In history, such visitors are often referred to as "pioneers," but in this situation you would probably be more likely to call me a burglar.

The first conversations between the people native to Europe and the people native to America must have been bewildering:

People Native to Europe: Excuse us, we've just arrived from Europe and we're pretty sure this is India.

People Native to America: No, this isn't India. It's somewhere else.

PNTE: We're going to call you Indians.

PNTA: We have our own names, thank you.

PNTE: We have some very fearsome weapons, and we insist.

This, of course, is probably not how it went at all. For one thing, the people native to America had likely not heard of India, so one could imagine it this way:

PNTE: This is India, right?

PNTA: What's India?

PNTE: A faraway place we were hoping to reach.

PNTA: Well, we don't call this place India.

PNTE: We're going to call you Indians.

PNTA: We have our own names, thank you.

etc.

but this is probably not how it went either, because the two groups of people did not speak the same language, so one can imagine it this way:

PNTE: ????

PNTA: ????

which is another way of saying that it was very difficult to imagine, even as I read, in *Everything You Know about Indians Is Wrong*, about the sadness and anger many people native to America feel to this day. The past can be as difficult to imagine as the future. It would be helpful in life, as in confusing books, to have an author, if that's the right word, explaining to us everything we find bewildering, in the hopes we all might feel better.

At last I reached the beekeeper, her table piled high with carefully labeled jars surrounded by other merchants selling all kinds of foodstuffs, a word which here means "things you eat." Our conversation went something like this:

Beekeeper: Why, hello, Mr. Snicket. I wasn't expecting to see you so soon. Did you run out of honey already?

Lemony Snicket: Good morning. I have plenty of honey, thank you. But I have reason to believe there was something amiss with my breakfast this morning, and I wanted to see if you had noticed anything that might be able to help me.

BK: Amiss?

LS: It's a word which here means "wrong."

BK: I know what "amiss" means, Mr. Snicket. But why do you suspect my honey?

LS: Well I don't, necessarily. For breakfast I had

Tea
with honey,
a piece of toast
with cheese,
one sliced pear,
and an egg perfectly prepared,

and I have reason to believe that poison may be lurking someplace in that list, so I am investigating as thoroughly as I can, at least until the poison takes effect.

BK: That seems sensible. I was afraid you might have been suspicious of the honey because of the name.

LS: What do you mean?

BK: Well, perhaps you don't know that *A Syrup of the Bees* is also the name of a book by the author F. W. Bain.

LS: I've read the book, actually, although I'm not sure "author" is the right word.

BK: I'm not sure there *is* a right word, Mr. Snicket.

I read that book when I was young, and I was quite fascinated with the old Sanskrit manuscript. But not until recently did I think to do some research on F. W. Bain, and I was bewildered to learn that there is no evidence whatsoever that *A Syrup of the Bees* or any of Mr. Bain's other books were translated from old manuscripts from India or anywhere else. I named my honey after a bit of trickery.

LS: Why did he do that?

BK: Well, these books were published in places where most people knew very little about ancient India or the people who lived there. I guess the stories seemed believable enough to some people, although plenty of people must have been confused, embarrassed or angry to read such nonsense. In any case, even if there is something amiss about F. W. Bain and his books, there's nothing amiss with my honey, Mr. Snicket. It's from the same bees as always, and they seem happy enough to let me take it and sell it, although I don't know that for sure, because of course I don't speak their language.

LS: Well, thank you for your help. I suppose I'll stop investigating my tea and move on to the foodstuffs in my breakfast.

BK: Not so fast, Mr. Snicket. You're forgetting an important ingredient in your tea.

LS: Which ingredient? Let me take out a scrap of paper and my pen, so I might write it down.

BK: I'll give you a hint,

and here she gestured behind her. I knew at once what she meant, and wrote it down: *water.* We were near the shore, and just a few blocks away was the beach, with great waves crashing against large rocks, and gulls squawking as they looked for food. I, of course, did not make my tea with seawater, but still I thanked the bee-keeper and bid her goodbye to walk the short distance to the beach. I stepped from rock to rock, avoiding the occasional crab, remembering one of F. W. Bain's notes in *A Syrup of the Bees* about the crabs of Ceylon, an island near India which is now called something else. "They run like the wind," he notes, "and jump over immense spaces and chasms, from rock to rock, better than any horse." Who knows if that is true, or if F. W. Bain had even been to Ceylon?

I stood on a rock as close to the waves as I dared. It is a spot I go to often, where the water is deep and cold and the air is busy with sound. It is a good place to swim, or just to think. The sea, like the lake where many years ago I had fed the geese, was all a case of knives, and I stared out at the glinting waves for quite some time.

Standing on the shore always makes me think of people who arrive in new places, particularly when travel was much more difficult and they did not know what to expect—people who left their native lands, for one reason or another, to arrive on the shores of someplace else. I come from such people. I belong to a tradition of people who feel displaced all the time, no matter which bewildering place we visit. I have written about some of these people, so perhaps you have read of the adventures and troubles they have had, when they left their homes behind and wandered this confusing and often frightening world. Perhaps you are one of us too, investigating your life and thinking about the world, always feeling native to nowhere. We put on disguises sometimes, to pose as people we are not, to hide, or to blend in, or just to see what will happen, hoping that our secrets will never be found out. We are scattered all over the world, and because we are scattered all over the world, we do not always understand each other. But people like us can try to imagine it, and try to feel like we are all in the same organization, or the same family, even if we do not even speak the same language.

The sea-birds squawked around me, and I remembered when the sorcerer Makarandiká from *A Syrup of the Bees* is married to Arunodaya, who believes she is the reincarnation of his wife from the pandit class, and says the wrong thing, wrecking her marriage and her life. She turns to her husband and says, "How short a time it seems, since I settled on that parapet in the form of a sea-bird," and he learns suddenly of her trickery, that she has spent years pretending to be something she is not. Why does she do this? I had thought that perhaps it made more sense in the original Sanskrit manuscript, but now I knew that there probably wasn't such a manuscript. I might never know anything more, I thought, never in my entire life, and who knew how short my entire life might be, due to poison?

The sea-birds settled together on a rock, and then flew around again, then settled, then flew around. I assumed they were native to the area, but for all I knew they were sorcerers. I did not know what they were called, and I did not even know what they were doing, flying and settling, settling and flying. I watched them for quite a while, wondering about my poisoned breakfast and all my unanswered questions, and knowing hardly anything about the birds in front of me. *They do that.*

I jumped into the water.

CHAPTER SIX

It is said that there are three rules for writing a book. The first rule is to regularly add the element of surprise, and I have never found this to be a difficult rule to follow, because life has so many surprises that the only real surprise in life is when nothing surprising happens. Perhaps you were surprised to read, at the end of the previous chapter, that I jumped into the cold and swirling water, which means I managed to follow the first rule of writing a book, but truth be told I was just as surprised to find myself plunging into the sea. It was the sort of decision you make so quickly it does not even feel like you are deciding, just that you have already decided. One moment I was standing on the rock, thinking of how if I were poisoned, I might not have many more chances to swim here at this particular spot, and the next I was in the water.

The second rule is to leave out certain things in the story. This rule is trickier to learn than the first, because while life is full of surprises, you can't leave any part of life out. Everything that happens to you happens to you. Often boring, sometimes exhausting, and occasionally thrilling, every moment of life is unskippable. In a book, however, you can skip past any part you do not like, which is why all decent authors try not to have any of these parts in the books they write. But few authors manage it. Nearly every book has at least one part that sits on the page like a wet sock on the ground, with the reader stopping to look at it thinking *What is this doing here?* This is why I left out the part where I removed most of my clothing before jumping into the sea, because no sensible reader is interested in things of that nature. If Little Red Riding Hood, the hero of an old folktale, needed to use the bathroom while walking through the forest to see her grandmother, that is her business, which is why just about all of the books about her leave out that part. If Oedipus, the hero of a famous play, had an itch he couldn't scratch and it really bothered him, that is not something we necessarily want to read about, so it should happen offstage where we won't hear about it. And I can't find a good reason to tell you exactly what I was wearing or if it required unbuckling or unbuttoning or if I folded things neatly or just dropped them in a heap on the rocks by the shore, so I have followed the second rule of writing a book, and left it out.

Of course, there are some parts of a story you can't leave out, or there is no story at all. I recently read of an old Japanese tale about a feudal lord, who, for some reason—it was left out of the story—hates old people, and so makes a rule that everyone over the age of seventy has to be brought to the mountains and abandoned there. One young man has an elderly mother, but he cannot bear to leave her in the mountains, and so hides her in the basement of their home. Soon afterward, some fierce enemies arrive and say that they will destroy the entire area unless the feudal lord can do three things:

1. make a rope of ashes,
2. pull a thread through a nine-sided jewel, and
3. cause a drum to beat by itself.

The feudal lord, of course, cannot do these things, but, the tale tells us, the mother can, and so everyone is saved and the feudal lord decides he doesn't dislike old people after all.

You can see at once that too much was left out of this story, and I was annoyed at whatever long-dead person had written it down without telling me how someone's mother managed to do the three seemingly impossible tasks of

    1. making a rope of ashes,
    2. pulling a thread through a nine-sided jewel,

and

    3. causing a drum to beat by itself.

If you leave this part out, I wanted to explain to this author, there is hardly any story at all, except for a vague lesson that we shouldn't hate old people, which all sensible readers know anyway. You can't hate old people, because if you are not an old person, you will become an old person, or die while trying to do so. So I will leave out the part about taking my clothes off—not every stitch of clothing, mind you, but just enough to swim and be decent at the same time—but I will keep in the book how it feels to me to swim in open water, a phrase which here means "not in a pool or a bathtub, but in a river or a lake or, best of all, the ocean," because it is important to the story and philosophy of this book.

Water and I have always gotten along. I was not a child who complained about having to take a bath or a shower, because I enjoyed being alone somewhere where people could not interrupt me, or if they did, I could pretend not to hear them over the water running. It was one of the delights of my childhood to say, over and over from my side of the bathroom door, "I'm sorry, I cannot hear you over the running of the water," even when I could often hear very clearly somebody or other saying, "Will you be much longer?" or "You must be clean by now" or "I think you're just turning the water back on every time I try to say something to you, Master Snicket." To this day, I like to sneak to a sink sometimes to splash water on my face, to wake myself up if I am feeling drowsy or to cool myself off if I am feeling cranky, and then to splash the droplets from my hands onto the mirror so it looks like the entire room is crying. I have always enjoyed a glass of water, something clear inside something clear, which seems to me full of hope. Sometimes when I am leaving my house, I decide to surprise myself by pouring myself a glass of water and leaving it on my desk for me to find a small gift from myself when I return, although sometimes, like the day I am writing about, I am in too much of a hurry to leave myself a surprise, so I tell myself, never mind me, I'll be fine when I get home, I'll explain to me that I didn't have time to leave me some water.

This morning I had hurried out of the house without even thinking about water, but now I was immersed in a body of water, which is my favorite kind. I like all sorts of ponds and lakes and seas and things. I like to stand at the edge of still water tossing pebbles, watching the little splashes and the circles spreading on the surface, always the same but different each time, like water itself, looking the same and different everywhere at once, the way an ocean will always be there but each wave will never happen again. I like to step slowly into a body of water, wading farther and farther in, the water getting deeper and deeper until I must give up walking and swim, but I also love to jump in and feel the sudden shift into being underwater, like the swift click into darkness when I turn the light off before bed.

Once I was in the water, I held absolutely still for a second, as I always do, as if waiting for something, which I was. I have always suspected that if and when my actual finest hour arrives, those perfect sixty minutes, I might be in a body of water, but of course I am always, in a way, in a body of water. The human body is about sixty percent water, more than half of each and every one of us. Being a body of water is something you can say about absolutely anyone, so if you are ever asked what a certain person is like, and you cannot think of anything nice to say, you can just reply, "They're mostly water." I lay there underwater, a body of water inside a body of water, and then began to move, feeling graceful and elegant even though I am not an especially impressive swimmer and I knew I was likely sputtering around gracelessly and inelegantly. I didn't care.

To some people, swimming in the ocean may seem very dicey, a word which here means "as risky as rolling dice, if getting a certain number means you will drown," and it is true you should never swim in a part of the ocean with which you are not familiar, because the tides and currents can behave like angry bus drivers taking you someplace far, far from where you want to go. There are also creatures in the sea, of course, and although most of them are harmless, you cannot regularly swim in the ocean without getting the occasional sting or nibble, the way you cannot

walk regularly in a park without getting some dirt on
your shoes, or attend school regularly without feeling,
one day or another, that you are all alone and nobody
likes you. Once I was swimming in the Pacific, one of
my five favorite oceans, and a sea lion bumped right
into me, very hard. We both stopped swimming and
looked each other in the eye. I understood at once the
sea lion's question—*Who are you and what are you
doing here?*—I hope the sea lion understood my silent
answer, which was, *I am a stranger and mean you no
harm.* Then, to my relief, we both went back to swimming, although in different directions.

There was no sign of any such beast now, though,
so I kept swimming, my ears getting used to the gurgle
of the water and my arms and legs finding a suitable
rhythm to keep myself moving, and then my favorite thing began to happen, the thing I like best about
swimming in open water, which is nothing. I don't
mean there is nothing to like. I mean there is nothing, and I like it. Even with all of the creatures and
the seaweed, the waves and the currents, the birds
and boats on the surface and the submarines and coel-
acanths somewhere down below, the ocean has a vast
emptiness, an immense open space that feels gaping
and vacant even though it is full of water. Swimming
in the ocean is like being a speck of dust in a large

empty suitcase, or one tiny star in the endless sky. Every thought you have feels unnoticed, the way the sky pays no attention to one star's flickering light, and every word in your brain echoes unremembered in the enormous suitcase of the sea,

so

you

stop

thinking

at

all.

A book of philosophy usually ends up talking about God, or whatever name anyone has for the author of the story of the world. People have wondered about this since people, and wondering, were invented. Countless books have been written on this topic, and no book will ever provide a definitive answer, a phrase which here means "solution that is so clear people will stop arguing about it." Some people think the story of the world has a very specific author, who is very opinionated about everything that is going on, and some people think the author has better things to do than worry about such events, and others think the story of the world has several or even many authors who are all working together or fighting or both. And some people think there is no author, and indeed the miracles of the world can seem even more impressive if you look at a meadow or a baby or some butterscotch syrup and believe that it all came from nothing.

There is a philosophical idea I have always liked called tzimtzum, which is as tricky to say out loud as it is to think about. Tzimtzum proposes that the world did come from nothing, but that the nothing was made by something, so something made nothing in order for something to come from the nothing, and this may be why we spend most of our lives drifting between nothing and something. Perhaps you find this confusing and might need to pause for a second to read that sentence again, and that is an important part of tzimtzum too. To think about something, you often need to pause first—to make nothing in your mind, just for a second, so there is room for you to think about what it is that has grabbed your attention. To think about something, you need nothing, just like whoever or whatever created the world, or, as one of my favorite writers once put it, "God made everything out of nothing, but the nothingness shows through."

This is a very deep sort of bewilderment, but I was in very deep water, and all this wondering about everything or nothing, someone or nobody, floated in my brain as my body of water floated in a body of water. They weren't quite thoughts, just little scraps of thinking, like the note about my poisoned breakfast, which was still in the pocket of my jacket neatly folded on the rocky shore, and from this I knew where I could go next, a place that might actually solve the mystery of my own poisoning.

It was strange that so clear a thought had come to me out of the blur of something and nothing, but that is often the way of the story of the world. Once I read a book that I admired very much, so much that I wrote a few notes in the margins of a few pages, something I only do when I am sure I will keep the book forever. I wrote things like "I like this" and "Yes, this is true" and "Look at this again" for me to find later when I reread it, much like the glass of water I occasionally leave for myself on my desk. Then years went by and I had a series of adventures. I moved from place to place, and I was forced to leave portions of my library in boxes, kept in closets and attics of various comrades and patient friends.

Finally, quite a few years later, I decided it was time to reread the book, but my copy couldn't be found—it was stuck in a box, probably, somewhere else. It was not a book that most bookshops happen to have on their shelves, so I had to search a little for a new copy of this book, and finally I found a library, in a part of the world I had never visited, which was selling some of its books to make room for new ones. There was a copy of the book I was looking for, and it was sent to me in a puffy brown envelope. I opened the envelope and then the book, and I saw there were some notes in the margins. It took me a few minutes to recognize my own handwriting, in the notes on the pages of my copy of this book that had somehow found me again. It was something so clear, my own notes to myself, out of the muddle of losing the book and looking for it again.

It was like one of many ideas I have had while swimming, that I hurry to write down, on any scrap of paper I can find so I will not forget it, as soon as I am out of the water and back on dry land. Every new idea is a fresh surprise, like finding my own book again after so many years, and the element of surprise, as I have mentioned, is the first of the three rules of writing a book. The second rule is to leave out certain things, which is why I did not add, to my story of finding my book, the very peculiar thing the author said to me when I tracked her down and told her what had happened, although I thought of it, as I pulled myself up onto the rock and shivered on the shore, leaving behind the bewildering nothing of my swim.

Nobody knows what the third rule is.

CHAPTER SEVEN

I sat on the shore shivering, which is how the body warms itself up. If you swim in cold water, you get used to the feeling of your body shaking and rattling, and the shaking and rattling view as you look at the world through shivering eyes. Eevvvvvven yyourrrr thoughtssss seemtoseemtoseemto shishishishiverververver forforforforfor awhiawhiawhilllle unununtiltiltil youyouyou've've've warmwarmwarmeded uuuppp enenoughough toto ththink clearly. But the idea in my head was as clear as the water I'd had it in, and I wrote it down in shaky handwriting as I shivered and waited for the wind to dry me.

The bewildering ocean, so busy and so empty at the same time, had reminded me suddenly of another busy and empty enormous place—the first place in my journey that actually seemed suspicious. The tea shop, even when closed, was a brave and unusual place, not suspicious at all, and the beekeeper seemed above reproach, a phrase which here means "too interested in uncovering the trickery of certain authors to slip poison into my honey," and my swim in the sea, although thrilling, was not going to uncover the story behind the terrible note I had received. There was too much water in the world to try and find the poison bit, particularly if I had already swallowed it. But there has always been something sinister to me about a supermarket.

I usually bought my usual bread for my usual toast for my usual breakfast—

Tea
with honey,
a piece of toast
with cheese,
one sliced pear,
and an egg perfectly prepared,

—at a supermarket, but I didn't like buying it there. As I have said, I prefer a shop which sells one thing to a shop which sells many things, and a supermarket, of course, tries to sell everything, and there is always something distrustful about a place so eager to please. I could have bought my bread at one of the two bakeries nearby, but the people at one of the bakeries move so slowly that I am always afraid the bread will be stale by the time they hand it to me, and the people at the other bakery are so mean I am always afraid I will have to use the bread to soak up my tears from hurt feelings. "I don't like your shirt," one of the workers at the second bakery said to me recently, handing me my bread and adding, "You should wear something else." I am not so fragile that I cannot stand to be criticized for my shirt, which that day was a very ordinary color with average buttons and regular stitching and a completely unremarkable collar, but for the next few days at breakfast, the loaf I had purchased appeared to be looking at me and shaking its floury head over my choice of clothing. Two years ago, meanwhile, I had asked for a loaf of pumpernickel at the first bakery, and the employee is still putting it into a bag. (I am exaggerating, of course, but not by much.)

The supermarket, on the other hand, had a sign on the outside that reads *Come On In!* which stared at me as I arrived. With its high-spirited exclamation point and friendly words, the sign was neither slow nor mean, and yet it seemed to me like something a dragon might put up outside its cave to lure passersby inside to be eaten. When I stepped inside, there were a few sentences painted on the wall that were so enthusiastic that I was wary, a word which here means "filled with unease no matter how many times I've read them." I reread the sentences for the umpteenth time, and copied them onto several scraps of paper, and I will write them here now, along with my unspoken thoughts as I read them, but I will not write the name of the supermarket in this book, in case my description is so upsetting that the grocers decide to get revenge.

Here at So-and-so Market, the wall began, *our primary concern is your happiness*, and the phrase "primary concern" was a creepy way of saying that it is the thing the market or wall is thinking about most. Happiness, in my experience, is like a bowl of bananas, because if you pay too much attention, it gets gobbled away, but if you forget all about it, either a robber steals it or it ends up rotten mush. It can be tricky to keep one's happiness intact, and the interference of a supermarket strikes me as only making things trickier. The sentences *Our primary concern is that our food is not spoiled* or *Our primary concern is that the floors*

aren't so slippery you will fall and break your leg or
*Our primary concern is that none of our bread has
been poisoned*, I thought, would be more welcoming.

We're here for you 24 hours a day, 365 days a year,
the wall continued, and this struck me as alarming,
because I didn't want a supermarket thinking about
me much more often than I thought about the supermarket. The supermarket should be thinking about
the delivery schedules of its trucks full of turnips
and noodles and duck, I thought, and whether the
back door has been propped open to admit poisoners,
instead of thinking about me, particularly late at night
when I might be tucked into bed telling myself that of
course there are no grocers peeking at me through the
curtains. I knew, of course, that the phrase *We're here
for you* did not necessarily mean that the supermarket was thinking about me, but just that it was there,
where So-and-so Street met Such-and-such Avenue,
whenever I might need groceries. But this also made
me wary, because promising to be there 24 hours a
day, 365 days a year, sounded not only exhausting but
unlikely. Someday the supermarket will close down,
because of bankruptcy or mice or an invading army,
and so this promise will be shattered along with the
wall on which it was written. I would have been more
reassured by sentences like *We're here, although you*

know this already because you're here too or *We have reasonable business hours* or *Goodness gracious, we hope nothing ghastly happens to this supermarket.*

Lastly, the wall said, *We consider each and every person who walks through these doors a friend*, and this I found the most bewildering sentence of all. I do not want to be friends with a supermarket or its wall. I want to be friends with people who are honest and interesting, generous but not ridiculous, thoughtful but who don't have irritating voices. You might use different words to describe the sort of people you want as friends, but I'm certain one of the words would not be "indiscriminate," which refers to people who'll be friends with absolutely anyone. You want friends who choose you, because they find you charming and fascinating, rather than just each and every person who walks through your door.

As I walked around the supermarket, I did not feel like a friend. I felt like a stranger, and I looked around at the other strangers, walking down aisles and peering into bins for whatever foodstuffs they wanted. There was music piped in—a phrase which here means "being played too loudly through speakers in the ceiling"—and it was another reason to be suspicious of the supermarket, because supermarkets usually choose music they think everyone will like, the way they think each and every person who walks through the door is a friend of theirs, and there is no such thing, of course, as music everyone likes. There is only music that some people think everyone likes, and I almost never like things some people think everyone likes. I do not like peanut butter and jelly sandwiches. I do not like paddling a kayak in the hot sun. I do not like Santa Claus. I do not like it when someone takes out a guitar and everyone has to sing. I do not like standing in a cheering crowd, particularly if the crowd is watching people whose job it is to throw a ball throw a ball. I do not like a picture of a man on a horse. I do not like it when everybody is doing the same thing and someone is standing with a stopwatch waiting to give a prize to the person who finishes doing it first. I do not like hot chocolate and I do not like wearing a shirt or a hat with the name of a place written on it so everyone knows you have been to that place, and I am not a fan of raisins, so I am often frowning at the music in the supermarket.

Surprisingly, however, the music that was playing right then was a piece of music that I liked very much. It is a very old song, so old that no one is sure who wrote it, and it has been sung by all sorts of people, although the version I prefer, the version that was play-ing in the supermarket, is sung by a woman who had

an adventurous and challenging life. The song is about
a man who has done something wrong. The song does
not tell us what it is, perhaps so we can fill it in with
our imagination or our memories of awful things we
have done ourselves, but the man is running and trying to escape from whatever wrong he has committed
and how terrible he feels about it. I walked from aisle
to aisle in the supermarket, listening to the woman
singing about the man and where he runs.

He runs to a rock, and then to a river and then the
sea, but he finds no comfort in any of those places.
Then he prays to God, and I remembered when I first
heard the song I thought I knew what would happen,
because usually a man in a song who prays to God
finds comfort. But the song follows not only the second rule of writing, which is leaving out certain things,
such as the wrong thing the man has done, but also
the first rule, which is to include the element of surprise, because instead of offering comfort God says to
him, "Go to the Devil," referring to an evil figure in
mythology and religion. The man goes to the Devil, as
God has suggested, and then the only thing the song
tells us is that the Devil is waiting, and nothing more.
There is something a little frightening about this, just
as there was something a little frightening about the
aisles of the store. The song seemed to be saying that

something evil has just been waiting while the man has been running around for so long, and now I saw food waiting everywhere, stuffed onto towering shelves and arranged into gigantic displays, the infinite sights and endless smells competing in the air, just waiting for someone to buy them. Knowing I had been poisoned made me feel queasy and anxious, so I was not hungry, and wandering amid such abundance, a word which here means "too much food," made me feel even more uncomfortable.

But truth be told, the abundance in supermarkets has always been bewildering to me. I stopped at a loaf of bread, for example, much like the one from which I had a toasted slice for breakfast. It was in a paper sack and gathered up with other identical loaves in a larger bag which was tucked into a basket, alongside many other baskets of bags of sacks of loaves of bread, next to a wall of high shelves with many, many more loaves, all in different bags and all with labels on the outside listing their ingredients.

The first ingredient in my bread was flour made from wheat, a plant I actually had growing in my tiny backyard. A friend had planted it for me as a gift, but only a little bit had sprouted, because I wasn't much of a gardener and didn't know how to make it thrive, a word which here means "grow tall and bushy

rather than shriveled and dead." Somewhere someone was a proper farmer, and somewhere was a bigger piece of land—much, much bigger—where people
were growing enough wheat to make all these loaves of
bread arranged before me, and all the extra loaves that
were likely in a refrigerator behind that door marked
No Admittance, a phrase which here means that you
can't go in, even though two people in aprons were
walking through it at that very moment. And think
of all the markets, I thought, super and not super, all
over the world with all their loaves of bread. Somewhere was enough land to grow all that wheat, but it
was impossible for me to imagine. Field after field of
wheat, stretching out as far as my mind could picture
them, but how could there be enough room for them,
and have there still be space on Earth for scorching
deserts and icy mountains and all the places wheat
cannot grow?

All that land was just for the wheat, and the wheat
was just for the flour. My bread had other ingredients,
and all the other breads had still more, salts and yeasts
and seeds and nuts and chemicals and additives har-
vested in marshes and picked in groves and cooked up
in laboratories and manufactured in factories. People
worked in all those places, making all those ingredients and mixing them together to make bread, and

someone made the label and the sack and the bag and the basket. Someone had loaded a truck, and driven it to town to be unloaded, and someone had arranged all the loaves in the supermarket, all to bring me this loaf of bread I would buy for a pittance, a word which here means "hardly any money." This pittance, of course, would be split among the grocers and the farmers and the label makers and all of the people I had imagined, plus all of the people I hadn't imagined and would never imagine. Surely it was not enough money for everybody. Surely someone was not getting enough money. I could imagine them living in poverty, maybe even starving, and yet there was so much bread, right here, that they might eat. The whole story was bewildering, and perhaps even cruel, and yet I did not want it to end. I did not want the supermarket to close down and stop selling its abundance. I liked this bread.

There is an expression from Persia, a part of the world which is now often called something else, that says, "When the cat and mouse agree, the grocer is ruined," presumably because if the cat didn't chase the mouse out of the store, the mouse would nibble on the groceries and perhaps frighten customers away, and the market would fail. If the mouse is happy, the grocer is suffering, and so for the grocer to be happy, the mouse has to suffer instead. For every creature who is happy and well fed, I thought, imagining the starving people while I stood surrounded by abundance, perhaps there is a creature who is hungry and ruined. No wonder, I thought, some people poison others.

The song, which was still playing, seemed to be saying that the wicked choice, the wrong thing you may have done, is easier to find than comfort and forgiveness, that it takes more effort to be a good person than a bad one, which might be why one sees wickedness in abundance, just sitting and waiting, while goodness is often so elusive, a word which refers to things that keep slipping away. This philosophical realization helped me put the bread down and slip away myself. If this were a story in a book, I thought, and the most suspicious place turned out to be villainous, then there would be no element of surprise. The thing to do, I decided as I left the supermarket, was to go to the least suspicious place instead.

CHAPTER EIGHT

I always feel hopeful when I step into a park. When a city or town sets aside a piece of land for public relaxation, it is a sign that someone is thinking about the happiness of someone else, that some people are trimming grass and sweeping pathways just so other people can have picnics and take walks or perhaps just sit and think. There are enormous parks with different areas for different activities, and there are parks so small they can fit under just one tall flagpole. There are parks full of devices and structures for playing, and parks full of flowers and trees for admiring, and parks full of statues and sculptures for appreciating, and parks full of garbage that really ought to be hauled away.

A proper park is open to the public, and when anything is open to the public, the public gets worried. If anyone is allowed into a place, then anyone might go there, and often there are all sorts of worried conversations about parks and the people who might cause trouble and activities that might upset people and times of day when a park should be one way and not another, and whether animals, who do not count as the public, will come into the park and mess it up or kill the flowers or bark too loudly or eat little children. But I like to use a park as the antidote to worry, rather than as an excuse to worry further, and I never mind whatever animals I see in a park. I've seen squirrels and chipmunks, snakes and salamanders, butterflies and ladybugs. I have seen dogs that look like foxes and foxes that look like dogs, and I have seen raccoons who look like burglars, although not yet any burglars who look like raccoons. I have seen, of course, many birds whose names I do not know, but I have also seen people whose names I do not know, runners and walkers, police officers on horses and horsey-looking people on bicycles, crying children with bored guardians and bored children with crying guardians, lost tourists with maps in their hands and kite flyers with string all over them, laughers and arguers and lovers, a word which here means "people who are kissing." Kissing is a common thing to see in parks, and this chapter contains more about kissing in a few pages, so if you are made uncomfortable by such things, you have now been fairly warned.

My favorite animals in this particular park, however, were not the lovers or the foxes or even the person selling popsicles in unearthly colors. My favorite were the goats. In this park there was a large herd of them employed as lawn trimmers, moved from field to field to feed on the grass so the sound of lawn mowers did not spoil the relaxation. The milk of the goats is also used to make cheese, and in fact the cheese I had on my toasted bread that morning was made from the milk of goats, so it made sense to continue my philosophical investigation by standing at the tilting fence for a few minutes, watching the goats and their goatherd, a word which here means "young man who always seems very bored looking after goats." I had spoken to this man once, and he'd admitted he was as bored as he appeared. I had suggested that he bring a book, one of those books that is interesting enough to keep you from being bored, but not so fascinating that you forget to look up from time to time to make sure the goats are safe, and he told me that he'd once brought such a book, and that the goats had eaten it. I waved at him now.

The goats, to judge from appearances, also looked bored, although I suppose it wasn't fair to judge by appearances. An associate of mine wrote a poem I like very much, which I thought of as I watched the herd wander around the meadow nibbling. The poem is called "300 Goats," after a large group of goats the poet is watching on a very cold day. "O lead them to a warm corner," she says to the goat rancher, using the letter O by itself which is always fun to write. "Lead them to the brush, which cuts the icy wind." But the goat rancher just shrugs at the poet's concerns. "They know what to do," the rancher says. "They're *goats*."

It is similar to the sentence the expert had said to me, when I had asked about the birds scrabbling around in the dirt: *They do that*, a simple and elegant summary of perfectly innocent behavior. I knew that this herd of goats, or indeed any herd of goats, would not be scheming to poison me, and that goatherds and cheese makers would not likely feel hostile toward a writer who regularly ate the cheese they'd made. They'd be more likely to poison the goats, I thought, for devouring their reading material, and so I turned my attention from the innocent goats and looked at some of the people around me.

Another interesting thing to do in parks, where so many different people may be seen, is to imagine what everyone is thinking and doing even though you will probably never know. At the other end of the meadow, two people were sitting on a scuffed-up bench, and as I walked toward an enormous tree, which rose straight up over a patch of gravelly ground, I imagined what the two people might have been saying to each other.

SYLVIA: Kiss me, Terry. O kiss me! Stop watching the goats and kiss me!

TERRY: Not now, Sylvia. And I'm not watching the goats. I'm watching that man walking toward the tree. Do you see him? His hair looks a little damp, as if he has recently been swimming in open water, and his eyes look a little haunted, as if he has recently been in a supermarket.

SYLVIA: Yes, I see him, Terry. He has a wistful expression on his face, as if he is remembering something happy that happened to him a long time ago.

I did not know what Sylvia and Terry, whose names, of course, I was imagining, were really saying, but they were correct in what I imagined they were imagining about me. I was in fact thinking of a time, a long time ago but in the exact same place I was standing. It is always strange to stand in a place where something happened to you long ago, particularly if the place has not changed much. The tree had surely grown a little, and the fence was perhaps more windblown and the benches a little scuffier than they were on that happy day, but it looks more or less the same, I thought, and I knew this because I had a photograph of the time I mean, the time I was thinking about.

The photograph was taken by someone I will never see again, and it shows me as a young man, so young that some people, to my annoyance, were still calling me a boy, sitting against the tree, my shoes resting on the gravel. You can see the bench in the background, where Sylvia and Terry were sitting, and indeed there are two people sitting on the bench in the photograph, although I don't know who they were, so of course I do not know where those people are now, or if the goats in the photograph were the same goats I was watching in the meadow. It seemed unlikely. It was a long time ago. The meadow was the same, and it was still right there in the park with me, but I did not know where anyone else from the photograph was. Sometimes when I look at the photograph, I think that moment was perhaps my finest hour, so long ago, and that I missed it, because I did not know it then. I don't look very happy in the photograph, although it was a happy day. Perhaps the person holding the camera just caught me at a moment where I was not displaying my happiness, or perhaps I did not quite know I was happy. You do not always know you are happy when you are happy. Sometimes you can't really tell when you are happy until it is over and you are thinking about it later. Next to me, in the photograph, is a young woman.

It is time here to say something about kissing, and remember you have been warned. There are some kisses that ought to come with warnings. I don't mean the sort of kissing that is done in families, where a child might get a kiss on the top of the head or the cheek with "good night." I don't mean a kiss blown into the air, toward an applauding crowd or a departing boat, or the kiss you might give an object, if it is important and you dropped it and it didn't break, or if it is just cold and smooth and feels good against your lips. You likely know the kind of kissing I mean, and you know how it is done, even if you have not done it yourself. It is done with two mouths, pressed together so that neither person can talk. It is a different kind of communication, this sort of kissing, than language, and although it is very important—practically nobody would be in the world if it weren't for kissing—it cannot last forever. Eventually you must take your mouth off the other person's mouth, and something is lost, when the kissing has to stop. The kissers become two people talking.

It does not matter, the story of what happened at the base of that tree. It has nothing to do with philosophy or with my poisoned breakfast, so I will leave it out. Like kissing, it is perhaps too powerful for words, even one "O" or a person's name. It can be very powerful to write the name of a person you have kissed or even just someone you wish you had kissed, on a scrap of paper where no one can see, or carved into the trunk of a tree where everyone can. It is even powerful just to write it down in your mind when you are alone, but it still does not matter, I thought to myself, because now I was alone there at the tree. When you are kissing someone, you feel perhaps that you will never be alone, but of course everyone is alone sometimes. It is lonely, sometimes, to be alone, but some people are good at being lonely. I am one of them. I am a loneliness savant, a word which here means that loneliness comes naturally to me, so I am quite good at loneliness, if I do say so myself. I like to think about lonely things, poems and philosophy and sad songs I admire, and places and people I do not know, or will never see again. It is said in a song I admire, by another associate of mine, that the loneliest people in the whole wide world are the ones you're never going to see again, and this is the sort of thing I like to think about: lonely thoughts and lonely language, and lonely things that happened, a long lonely time ago, things that you tell yourself, walking on the gravelly ground under a tree that has been there for a long time, do not matter. Telling yourself that something does not matter is one of the loneliest things you can do, because you only say it, of course, about things that matter very much. But often, and this is the lonely part, they only matter to you.

SYLVIA: O!

TERRY: What happened?

SYLVIA: I think that man, while thinking about lonely things that only matter to him, tripped and fell into the gravel.

CHAPTER NINE

I lay face down under the tree, wondering if I was dead, or at least dying, of poison. If I had to die—and of course, I did, either right then or some other time—it was not a bad place for it. I thought it could even be a pleasant place for a funeral, and perhaps I could even be buried underneath the ground underneath the tree where I was apparently dying. I did not want to die, of course, but it seemed useless to worry about it happening now that it was happening. "Why oh why didn't I treat Lemony Snicket better?" I could almost hear someone wailing, at my elegant funeral.

But after a few moments I could tell that I wasn't dead, not right then. My body did not feel poisoned. It was not shaking or shivering or heaving like a malfunctioning washing machine. I could feel, here and there, some nasty scrapes from my fall, but I could tell I had no serious injuries, no broken bones or major sprains or a concussion, a word for the alarming things that happen if you hit your head too hard. I hadn't. I wasn't dead and I wasn't seriously injured. I was just sore and embarrassed, which is something that often happens when you are clumsy.

If you are a clumsy person, you will bang some part of your body, or get it caught and pinched in something, or have something twisted around the wrong way because you have done the wrong thing because you are clumsy. It will hurt, so you will be sore, and it is likely someone will be looking at you, wondering how on earth you managed to bang or catch or pinch or twist yourself doing something that everyone else does all the time without incident, so you will be embarrassed. A peculiar thing about being embarrassed is that once you have decided you are embarrassed, you become less embarrassed, so I just lay there, knowing I was embarrassed and deciding not to be embarrassed about being embarrassed and getting less and less embarrassed as I lay there with my face in the little rocks.

There is another thing that happens if you are clumsy, which is more interesting than being sore or embarrassed, and that is you get to see things most people don't. Being clumsy treats you to views of the world of which graceful people never get a glimpse. If you are in an art gallery, for instance, and scrape your leg against something that everyone else has managed to walk around, you will get to see the gallery's back room, where they store strange sculptures and bandages. If you drop a rolling pin in someone's kitchen, you will see an interestingly shaped smudge of butter and flour most people never see, not to mention the drawer where rags are kept, and if you drop the rag you will see what it looks like bunched up under the kitchen table, and when you bang your head on the kitchen table you will get a close-up view of a towel with ice inside of it as you hold it against your head to reduce swelling.

I was appreciating a close-up view of gravel, which graceful people walk on all the time without ever knowing what it looks like pressed up against their faces. It was an interesting sight, fragments of limestone and basalt, which were the kinds of tiny rocks looming in front of my eyes like boulders, and then I turned over and lay on my back looking straight up at the tree. That was a much more interesting view, if a little dizzying, with the branches and leaves hanging over me like drifting thoughts, and I was grateful for my clumsiness which showed me something I had never noticed about the tree, after years of walking past it, something that made me think I might be closer to learning more about the mysterious and menacing message in my pocket. I looked at what I was seeing, and then I had to blink again, because my view was blocked by a man leaning over to ask me what happened.

"What happened?" he asked.

"At first I thought I was dying," I said, "but it was just that a fragment of either limestone or basalt rolled under my foot as I stepped on it, which made my left foot slide slightly. I tried to move my right foot in the proper direction to regain my balance, but additional fragments of limestone and basalt interfered by rolling further. By then, my arms were splaying out like the wings of an airplane, in an attempt to distract the force of gravity from catching me in its claws, but I miscalculated and fell into a heap under this tree."

"In other words," the man translated, "you are clumsy."

He extended his hand and I took it, and he helped me to my feet. "That is an elegant translation of what I just said," I told him, brushing gravel off my clothing. Off in the distance I could see Sylvia and Terry, who were not, of course, Sylvia and Terry, sitting on their bench, and the goats wandering the meadow. The man talking to me was wearing a suit the color of a day threatening rain, though his smile was quite sunny. "It's funny you should say that," he told me. "I'm a translator by trade."

"A translator?" I said in surprise.

"Yes, I take pieces of writing in one language, and rewrite them in another," he said, "so that more people can read them."

"Translation is noble work," I said. "What sort of writing do you translate?"

The man looked at me and his smile got sunnier, and then he said one of my favorite words in the world. It is a word that comes from Latin, an ancient language nobody speaks anymore unless they are trying to show off, which means someone translated it, long ago, so that I could have this word in my life. It is a little difficult to say why this word is so important to me. It is just a word for books and writing, but it is a word which conveys respect and admiration and hope. The respect is for the words themselves and the power that even a simple word—the word "poison" for example—can carry. The admiration is for how the authors put words together, in books you love the most. And the hope is that these sorts of words and these sorts of authors will continue to be read as time goes by. They will not always be the same words and the same authors, but they will stay with us, we hope, the way the meadow will have different goats, and the tree will have different fruit on its branches, but the park will still be there and people will still be there to see it. When you say the word, you are giving books and writing all this respect and admiration and hope, and so it is like calling your favorite books by a special name. It is a word that raises books and writing closer to the sky, and it raises all of us that way just to say it. It was almost a shame, I thought, that this wasn't the moment of my death, because if there had to be a word that was my last—and there did, either right then or some other time—it wasn't a bad one.

"Literature," is what he said.

"Literature," I repeated.

"Literature," the translator agreed. "In fact, I was just walking here with an author whose books I have translated from another language into the one we are speaking now. We were telling each other stories when

we saw you fall into the gravel. If you're a fan of literature, perhaps you'd like to meet him."

"I would be delighted," I said, and the translator
led me down the path to where the author was waiting, dressed in colorful and old-fashioned clothing. I
do not speak the author's language and the author did
not speak mine, but the translator, naturally, spoke
both languages, and conveyed our greetings in the language we could each speak. You might think that it
would feel clumsy, having a conversation in which only
one person understood every word and had to keep
repeating each sentence in two different languages,
but the translator did it very gracefully and our talk
went quite smoothly.

"I always enjoy having conversations with authors
I am translating," said the translator, translating as he
went, "because reading a book makes me feel as if I
am in conversation with the author."

"I often feel the same way when I am reading," I
agreed.

"So when you read a book which has been translated from another language," the author said, with
the translator helping me understand it, "it is a conversation like this one, with the translator helping
you along."

"Quite so," the translator said. "I'm happy to be of assistance in literature or in life."

"Well then," I said, "perhaps you can assist me with this," and I reached into my pocket and took out the note—

You had poison for breakfast

—and waited while the translator read it and told the author what it said. I do not know why I showed them the note, when I hadn't shown it to my neighbor or the beekeeper or anyone at the supermarket, but perhaps it was the word "literature" which gave me the courage to share such a strange piece of writing. The author listened to the translator's words and then raised his eyebrows and replied.

"This note follows the two rules of writing a book," the translator translated.

"I thought there were three rules," I said.

The author shook his head when he had understood what I'd said, and raised two fingers, a gesture which the translator left in its original language.

"The first rule is to include the element of surprise," I said, "and the second is to leave things out."

"Those are the same thing," the author explained, with the translator's help. "A surprise becomes unsurprising if you have an explanation, so a writer must leave certain things out to keep the surprise surprising. If a book begins, *The girl walked toward a door behind which a monster was hiding*, the author would have already spoiled the surprise. If you leave out the monster, and begin with merely *The girl walked toward a door*, then the reader will be as surprised as the girl when the monster appears. Your two rules are really two translations of the same single rule."

"I never thought of it that way," I said. "So the first rule is simply, be surprising."

"Excuse me," the translator said, "but I'm not sure *surprising* is really the right word. As a translator, I think something more dramatic and complicated is in order."

Thinking up the right word, of course, is part of an author's job, and both authors tried to be of assistance.

"*Startling?*" I suggested.

"*Startling* seems too jumpy," the translator said, in one language and then another.

"*Stunning?*" the author suggested.

"*Stunning* seems too happy," the translator said.

"*Astonishing?*"

"*Confounding?*"

"*Flooring?*"

"*Stupefying?*"

"*Staggering?*"

"*Flabbergasting?*"

The author and I kept suggesting words in both our native languages, but none of them seemed quite right to the translator, until one of us supplied a word that this book, as I've said, is really about.

"*Bewildering,*" someone said, and everyone else grinned in agreement.

"The first rule is about bewilderment," the author said, although of course he was referring to the word in his language rather than mine, "and of course nobody knows what the second rule is."

"I certainly don't," I said, "and I don't know much about this note, either, although I've spent the whole morning trying."

"Just the word *poison* is powerful," the translator said, looking at the note again, "although poisons themselves aren't necessarily powerful either. Let me tell you a story. Some years ago I treated myself to a cactus at a cactus shop in my neighborhood. I kept it in my office where the afternoon sun shines very brightly through my windows, and the cactus grew very tall and prickly. I was quite proud of it. But one day, I damaged my cactus."

"How did you do that?" I asked.

"I was putting a dictionary back on a high book-shelf," the translator said, "when my thumb slipped and knocked a little brass tiger off the neighboring shelf. I reached down to try to catch the little tiger, which I had treated myself to at a garage sale some years previous, but my shoulder bumped up against another shelf where a fascinating twelve-volume diary had been arranged rather carelessly, so volume seven fell on my toe, causing me to drop the dictionary onto the cactus which bent suddenly and horribly toward the ground."

"In other words," I translated, "you are clumsy."

The translator smiled ruefully, a word which here means "wishing he didn't have to agree." "I'm clumsy," he agreed, "and the cactus was quite banged up. There was a large hole in its main cladode, which was leaking fluid onto the floor."

The author said what turned out to be the equivalent of "I'm sorry to hear that."

"Immediately, I picked up the cactus," the translator said, "and left my office to hurry toward the cactus shop. The cactus was in a pot, of course, but I had to hold the plant itself so it wouldn't bend any further and break in half. The fluid was spreading on my hands and some of the spines of the cactus pricked me, so I occasionally put a finger or thumb into my mouth to numb the pain. I could taste the fluid of the cactus, which was sweet and warm."

"I've eaten cactus myself," the author said in his own language, "in an omelet with a woman who wouldn't stop crying."

"The cactus merchant was practically crying when she saw my wounded plant," the translator said. "She said she would try to save it as best she could, but that it would probably die. But then she looked at my prickled fingers and asked me in a worried tone if any of the cactus fluid had gotten on my hands or in my mouth, and I said of course it had. After all, I had carried the wounded cactus for several blocks. She sighed sadly and told me that it was a poisonous cactus."

The author and I both gasped, which did not need translation.

"I asked the cactus merchant what I should do about it," the translator said, "and she said there was no antidote to the poison. She told me that even if I went to the best nearby hospital there was nothing anyone could do. I told her there must be something, and she said there was no hope whatsoever. 'The poison,' she said, 'must run its course. For the next hour or so, your hands and mouth will itch slightly and then it will be over.'"

The author and I breathed a sigh of relief and laughed. "So you were fine?"

"Poisoned," he said, "but fine."

"That story bewildered me," the author told him.

"I'm flattered," the translator said.

"It's a puzzling story," I agreed, "but I do find it helpful to remember that some poisons are more dangerous than others."

"I'm happy to be of assistance," the translator said, "in literature or in life."

"It's some of the first real assistance I've had since breakfast," I said, "which was

Tea
with honey,
a piece of toast
with cheese,
one sliced pear,
and an egg perfectly prepared,

and I noticed for the first time, that this tree, where I often walk and occasionally fall, grows pears just like the one I had for breakfast. I had never noticed it before. Do you think it means something?"

The three of us walked back to the tree and stared up at the pears, some of which were hanging just a few inches over our heads, reminding me of an expression, "low-hanging fruit," which can refer to the easiest thing to do, often when there are more difficult things ahead.

"Pears can be the source of all kinds of mysterious things," the author said. "Let me tell you a story. A long time ago, there was a merchant selling pears in a marketplace. A traveling monk asked if he could have one, but the merchant refused. The monk was dressed in tattered clothing, and the other market goers felt very sorry for him and began urging the merchant to give one single pear from his abundance. The merchant refused, so finally someone purchased a single pear and gave it to the monk, who gobbled it up, leaving behind a single seed. As the crowd watched, the monk planted the seed in the ground, and within moments it had grown into a pear tree covered in fruit which the monk distributed to the crowd. The pear merchant watched all this in fascination and frustration, and then suddenly noticed that all of his pears were gone. Suspecting the monk of trickery, the merchant turned to confront him but the monk, too, had disappeared."

"What a bewildering story," I said. "Why did the monk ask for a pear if he could grow them himself? Or did he steal the merchant's pears and somehow make it look as if they had grown magically?"

The author did not answer me, and at this point I will tell you something that perhaps you have already suspected, so it will not be much of a surprise. I have told you that everything in this book is true, and it is. It is also true that I was still lying on the gravel, looking up at the tree and thinking, and it is true that I was alone. The tree, I had noticed from my clumsy view, was a pear tree, which reminded me of the pear I had for breakfast, which naturally made me think about poison, and then, suddenly, I remembered my wounded cactus and my brief panic when my cactus merchant had told me I was poisoned. But the pears had also reminded me of the story I just told you that the author had just told me. The story of the pear merchant was from a book, written in another language a long time ago and translated fairly recently. I have never met the author, probably because he died hundreds of years before I was born, and neither have I met the translator, possibly because he is avoiding me, but reading a book makes me feel as if I am in conversation with the author, often assisted by a translator, and so I entered into a conversation as I lay in the gravel thinking about a poisoned cactus and a pear merchant and if including the element of surprise is really the same as leaving certain things out, the way someone going on a journey might really be the same story as a stranger coming to town, if the only story is really somebody loses something and the only rule is to be bewildering, besides, of course, the rule nobody knows. Life is like this, and literature, imaginary conversations and true stories mingling like languages in translation.

I thought all this lying there underneath the tree, looking at the low-hanging fruit. The easiest thing to do was to stop thinking about the pear I'd eaten for breakfast. As the author and translator had reminded me, pears can be the source of all kinds of mysterious things, and if I kept thinking about them I might spend the rest of my life, however short that might be, lying on the gravel without ever knowing if my pear was poisoned, and after a few minutes the gravel was too uncomfortable to lie on any longer. I stood up, all by myself, and looked around. There were more difficult things ahead. I had to keep moving, to keep thinking and telling stories, and I set out for one last place I could go, before the poison overtook me and my story would be over.

CHAPTER TEN

Philosophy has been called the pursuit of truth and wisdom, and "pursuit" is a word which refers to chasing after something, but of course you do not chase after truth and wisdom the way you chase after a tennis ball rolling down the driveway or an executive who has stolen your hat. The pursuit of truth and wisdom instead requires asking questions, and this part of the book asks one of the most famous and most difficult philosophical questions. It was the question I was asking myself as I left the park, jittery from the imaginary conversation I have reported exactly as it happened. You have likely heard the question yourself, although perhaps no one told you it was philosophical. The question is, "Which came first, the chicken or the egg?"

If you walked around one day asking people this question, some people would say that the chicken came first, because chickens lay eggs, and some people would say that the egg came first, because eggs hatch into chickens. But most people would just tell you that they did not have time for such nonsense. All of the most important questions in life are dismissed most of the time by most of the people, and it is true that much of the world prefers to do something more practical, such as raising children, or moving a chair to a certain part of the room, or writing themselves a note on a scrap of paper so they remember to buy a new shower curtain, than to sit and think about which came first, the chicken or the egg. But something happens when you think about these enormous questions. As you imagine, for instance, a chicken emerging from an egg which has emerged from a chicken which has emerged from an egg, your mind wanders as if on a voyage, and as with any voyage, you are likely to discover something along the way. It is almost as if enormous philosophical questions are not designed to be answered at all, but just to make you think. I thought about the egg I had eaten that morning, a perfectly prepared egg, and it occurred to me, walking down a twisty street, that if I put my mind to the question, "Which came first, the chicken or the egg?" I might discover the source of my poisoned breakfast as I walked closer to the last place I would visit.

I enjoy eating eggs, and eggs look so cheery on a breakfast plate that I cannot help but think that eggs enjoy being eaten. I have often thought that it would be pleasant to be a chicken because whenever I was in the mood for an egg I could just sit down and make one for myself, although I suppose wishing I was a chicken means wishing I was first an egg, and I don't think I would enjoy breakfasting on my own childhood.

It upsets some people to eat anything that comes from an animal, which is a good reason for not eating eggs. Another reason is being severely allergic to eggs, because, as I did not need to be reminded that morning, it is no fun to worry about death right after eating breakfast. Some people, however, say that they do not eat eggs because they do not like them. This is suspicious. Eggs are tremendously flexible and can be prepared in a variety of ways, all of which are different experiences in one's mouth. If you say you do not like eggs, it is like saying you do not like books or light or wearing a ball gown. It means you simply have not found the right kind.

My breakfast egg was perfectly prepared, as I have said, and there are five basic methods of preparing eggs. Each method has something of a trick to it, and it is useful to have a trick when learning to do something. I have memorized tricks for doing things I hardly ever get to do, just because the trick is so handy. I always remember the sentence "A rat in the house may eat the ice cream," for instance, as a trick for spelling the word "arithmetic" by using the first letter in each word in the sentence. I have hardly any call to spell the word "arithmetic," but when it happens, I am ready with the trick. Similarly, I have learned the trick for each basic egg preparation method, and I went through them in my mind as I continued to walk.

The first way eggs can be prepared, and the most popular, is scrambled. "Scrambled eggs" is a phrase which here means "eggs taken out of their shell, mixed up, and cooked in a pan," and the trick with scrambled eggs is never to eat them. Scrambled eggs are unreliable, a word which here means that you never know what scrambled eggs will be like, whether you make them yourself or convince someone else to make them for you. Scrambled eggs can be runny, a word as disgusting to read as it is to experience, or lumpy, as if they have been punched by a hammer or some deranged person. Scrambled eggs cool down very quickly, so they can be cold, and once you have eaten a bite of cold scrambled eggs it can take you a year to recover, but scrambled eggs also burn easily, so you may find something in your mouth that feels like the blazing sole of an old shoe. Scrambled eggs can make more than one of these mistakes, or even all at once, and the world knows this, which is why scrambled eggs often have other, more reliable things in them, such as cheese or tomatoes or oysters or onions, so that scrambled eggs become much more delicious dishes, like covering up your ugly underwear with a handsome pair of slacks, all because scrambled eggs are so dangerously unreliable. I have a dear friend who once ordered scrambled eggs at a restaurant, despite my repeated warnings. They arrived at the table not at all to her liking, and she asked the cook to prepare them again, and then again, and again. The cook grew angry, I grew embarrassed and my friend grew hungrier and hungrier, and all this could have been avoided if she had never uttered the words "Scrambled, please."

The second way eggs can be prepared is fried, and the trick to fried eggs is to remember the words of a great composer. The composer I am thinking of wrote music that is very slow and quiet, and once when asked about his method of composing music, he replied that he never moved the notes around. "Not even a little bit?" he was asked, and he said no, not even a little bit. I do not know what this means, not even a little bit, but to make fried eggs, put a little butter in a pan and place the pan on something very hot, such as a flame. When the butter melts, crack an egg open and dump the insides in, tossing the shell someplace else. Then, remembering the composer's bewildering words, do not move it around, not even a little bit. Cook the egg until the white part stops looking gleamy but the yellow part is still bright and sunny. Some people like to flip the egg over at this point, presumably because they prefer eating something that looks speckled and greasy instead of something that looks like a sunrise. Do not trust these people. If they were composers, they would probably move the notes around.

The third way eggs can be prepared is poached, a word which here means "simmered and delicious," and the trick to poaching eggs is to add a bit of vinegar to the water. Vinegar is a strong-smelling liquid which has a magical effect on a poached egg. To experience this magic, boil water in a small pot and then add a bit of vinegar. Then, crack an egg into a small cup, and, using a spoon, create a sort of whirlpool in the boiling water where the egg will go. The water cooks

the egg and the vinegar makes it fluffy, so that eating a poached egg is like having a moon, shrouded in
clouds, for one's breakfast. One of the truest things I
know is that if you do not like a poached egg, there is
something wrong with you.

The fourth way eggs can be prepared is baked, and
the trick to baked eggs is that you must burn your fingers. If you are a concert pianist or just enjoy pointing
at people, you should have your baked eggs prepared
by others, so that your fingers remain attractive and
useful. The rest of us should turn on an oven to a high
temperature and read a few pages of a book until the
oven has heated itself up. Then, an egg can be emptied
into a ramekin, a word which sounds like a nickname
for your favorite sheep but is actually a small ceramic
container which gets very hot in an oven. This is what
you will burn your fingers on. Place the ramekin in
the oven until the egg looks like something you want
to eat. Turn off the oven and remove the ramekin,
burning your fingers while you do so even if you are
wearing an oven mitt. Eat your baked egg while crying
and nursing your fingers, knowing that it happens to
anyone who prepares a baked egg. There is no trick to
stop yourself from burning your fingers, only the trick
of telling yourself that this terrible thing will certainly
happen from time to time.

The last way eggs can be prepared is boiled, and the trick to preparing a boiled egg is to remember that you will die. Boil water in a pot, and this is the world. Put an egg in the pot, and this is you. Prick it with a pin first, but do not worry, because the egg will not remember this, just as you do not remember your life before you were in the world. The hole made by the pin keeps the egg from cracking under pressure, which some eggs—and some people—occasionally do.

Once the egg is in the pot of boiling water, you must watch over it holding a slotted spoon. You are the figure of Death. The egg does not know how long it will be in the world, before the great spoon of Death will lift it away. Perhaps it will be a long time, because someone wants a hard-boiled egg, which is good at a picnic or to startle someone by tossing it at them. Or perhaps it will be a short time, three minutes perhaps, and enjoyed in an egg cup, a phrase for a cup which holds an egg. You can eat it with a tiny spoon, alongside a sliced pear, a piece of toast with goat's-milk cheese, and a cup of tea with honey, and enjoy all this while reading, never knowing if it is your last breakfast, if today is the day you will be spooned out of the world, but hoping that you, like the egg, are perfectly prepared.

I had been thinking all this time about eggs, but now I turned my attention to thoughts of chicken, even though chicken can be prepared in the same basic ways, with the same tricks. Boiled chicken makes a healing soup when you are sick and wondering if you are going to die. You will burn your fingers while baking a chicken, and a properly poached chicken will taste a little fluffy. Fried chicken should not be moved, and it lies so heavily in the stomach that you will not want to move after you eat it, not even a little bit, and the trick to scrambled chicken is not to have any.

As I had suspected, all this thinking about the chicken and the egg had not helped me answer the question of which came first. But it had taken me on a journey, as I had hoped it would. For one thing, I realized my egg had been perfectly prepared, as I have been reminding you every few pages. A perfectly prepared egg would not contain poison, and even if it did, it would likely drain out of the pinhole while the egg was being boiled. But this was a very small realization compared to the enormous sea of philosophy in which my poisoned head was swimming. My jittery mind had surrendered to a longer, quieter way of thinking, a way of discovering something other than the answer to an unanswerable question.

I remember very clearly the first time I knew I was thinking this way. I was led there by a book, one of the greatest books that has ever been written. The book is something of a mystery, although it is also something of a book of philosophy, with enormous questions and small sentences of truth and wisdom written on scraps of paper. In my favorite part, a girl begins thinking about the world, in the hopes of solving the mystery around her, and she closes her eyes and imagines herself in a dark cave, on a path taking her deeper and deeper inside, which is how investigating a mystery can feel. When she can imagine herself going no further, she rounds a corner and sees, in the cave, a tiger, sitting on a blanket. The tiger doesn't say a word, and she wonders if this tiger is the source of the mysterious world in which she is living. *God?* she thinks to herself, and then wonders, *Then who made the blanket?*

The first time I read this book I was quite young, and when I reached the sentence *Then who made the blanket?* I blinked, and the girl and the tiger and the cave all vanished. I was no longer in the world of the book, which had changed the landscape around me. I was in the world I was in, reading in bed, one hand holding the book and the other clutching my bedcovers. I looked down, away from the sentence *Then who made the blanket?* and looked at my blanket and wondered who made it. And that moment, for the first time I can remember, I understood that I knew nothing, that all the tiny things in my mind were just little tricks, as far from truth and wisdom as vinegar is from the question of whether the chicken or the egg came first. I knew nothing at all, from who made the blanket which was lying over me to why I was sneaking out in the mornings to give a secret breakfast to the birds by the water. In short, I was bewildered, but at least I had a book in my hand, and I knew where the book came from. I knew it now. I hadn't solved the mystery of my poisoning, not yet, but I knew where I was going and what I might do to learn more.

I arrived. I walked up the steps. I opened the door, and I entered the library.

CHAPTER ELEVEN

It is difficult for me to exaggerate how much I love a library. It is not impossible, of course, because I am a writer, and writers can exaggerate anything. If I wrote that I loved libraries so much that if I were in a building on fire, and only had time to save either a scrap of paper with the word "library" written on it or the three hundred people I love most in the world, that I would choose the scrap of paper, that would be an exaggeration, because of course I would save all of those frightened people. But as I led them to safety, I would be a little sad that the word "library" would be reduced to ashes, because I love a library. Just to walk inside one, and to breathe in a room where so much literature has been gathered, is such a powerful feeling that it often brings a tear to my eye, although that could also be my mild allergy to dust.

I walked in and looked around. It was still morning and the library had not been open long, so there was a sense of readiness among the books on the shelves. Their spines were lined up neatly, in every color and width that could be imagined, like a team of comrades ready to snap into action. The numbered labels looked precise and eager to be of service. There were books on all sorts of topics, from exciting things of vital importance to things that nobody had reason to care about, but in a library the topics keep taking turns being important or interesting. Each patron in a library is looking for something different, and so the book you hardly notice is the book someone else is breathless to find, and the book that always makes you smile is busy making someone else sick. As someone who writes books, this always gives me hope. Some book of mine—this book of philosophy, for example—may sit ignored and lonely on a high shelf, but then someday a reader will walk into a library and spot the spine of the book they have been waiting for, and they will pluck my book off the shelf and use it to stand on, to reach the book they are excited to read.

Books, however, are just one part of a library. A proper library has at least one fantastic librarian, preferably more than one, so if the fantastic librarian goes out to lunch or falls into a tar pit, there will be a spare. A fantastic librarian can help you find what you are looking for, and not just if it is a book. A fantastic librarian can help you find a hobby or an occupation, a cure or a challenge, a quiet fact or a loud opinion, or a small town where you might hide for months. A fantastic librarian knows more about what you are looking for than you do, the way a cookie in a bakery knows you want to eat it before you even know it is out of the oven, and like a good cookie, a fantastic librarian doesn't show off about it, just waits silently for you to open your mouth. I was a little ashamed of myself for not thinking earlier I should go to the library to investigate my sinister note, but I comforted myself by remembering that the library was not open early in the morning, presumably so the fantastic librarians can eat a hearty breakfast to gather their strengths. I saw my favorite librarian right away, and she hates so much to show off that she doesn't want her name in these pages, so for the purposes of this book I am identifying her as the great American poet Emily Dickinson. She is not, of course, actually Emily Dickinson, who is dead and was rumored to have been such an odd person that she likely would not have made a good librarian, but in this book, she is quite alive and very capable, and I was very happy to see her.

"Good morning, Ms. Dickinson," I said. "I'm happy to see you."

"I'm happy to see you too, Mr. Snicket," replied the poet. "How might I be of assistance? From where I'm sitting, you look a little worried."

Where Emily Dickinson was sitting was an elegant wooden desk, donated to the library from a bank that closed down about a hundred years after her death. She shut a book she was reading, and looked at me expectantly, as I took out the message and pushed it across the desk for her to read.

You had poison for breakfast.

I watched her eyes sweep across the scrap of paper more than twice. A fantastic librarian reads everything two times at least.

"You've brought me a great number of bewildering slips of paper," she said, "but this might be the most bewildering yet."

"I would prefer not to die," I told her, "so I've spent all morning thinking about it."

"Well, that seems like a big part of your occupation, Mr. Snicket. Isn't it? You walk the streets, usually with a book and some scraps of paper in your pocket, thinking about things and writing them down, and sooner or later you end up in a library."

"It's true," I said. "Today I left my house to follow a stranger, but he vanished. I visited a tea shop, but it was closed. I talked to my beekeeper, and she pointed me toward the water. I jumped in the water and thought of the supermarket. I escaped the supermarket and went to the park. I fell in the park and had a conversation. The conversation was imaginary so I asked a question. But the question had no answer, and all the while I kept thinking and writing notes to myself, and I'm not sure one scrap of it has been of any use whatsoever."

"That is one of the frustrations of a life spent in literature," the librarian said ruefully, gesturing to the books which were surrounding us. "Countless writers express countless ideas on so many bits of paper, and at some unknown moment some specific book, even some specific sentence, will be the right one for the right person. We never know when some scrap of literature will have its finest hour."

"So what do we do?" I asked, as countless readers have asked one another.

"We keep reading," the librarian said firmly, "and it just might be our turn to triumph." She handed me my scrap of paper and opened the book she was reading. "I've spent all morning with the story of a composer who triumphed over much more troubling circumstances than yours, Mr. Snicket."

"The composer who never moved the notes around, even a little bit?"

"No, not that one," said Emily Dickinson. "This composer's music is very moving indeed, and I've just learned the story of how my favorite of his pieces was written. The composer had been captured by an army and was forced to live in a prison camp. In that terrible place he met three other musicians, and using a broken pencil and some old paper given to him by a prison guard, wrote a piece of music for the four of them to play together. Somehow they found instruments— a violin, a cello, a clarinet and a piano, all terribly damaged—and organized an outdoor concert. The day of the concert, it was pouring rain, but they performed this new, strange piece for an audience of hundreds of prisoners and guards who gathered to hear it." She flipped pages in her book until she found what she was looking for. "Do you know what the composer said about that day, Mr. Snicket?"

"I cannot imagine," I said.

"I couldn't either," the librarian said. "I can't really imagine what a prison camp is like. I've read books and I've seen pictures, so I know that prison camps usually consist of a group of buildings or tents that are heavily guarded and very uncomfortable. Prisoners sleep all crowded together, and all day long are forced to do exhausting labor, and there is hardly enough food to go around. But I can't imagine it, really. I cannot truly picture a place where a simple writing implement cannot be found, or where hundreds of people would stand in the rain to hear four musicians play on battered instruments."

"I can't either," I said. "Tell me what he said."

Emily Dickinson nodded, and read out loud from the composer's story. "*Never was I listened to with such rapt attention and comprehension,*" she said. "That means everyone was listening very closely, and everybody understood his music like they never had before." She shut the book and gazed down at it in admiration. "It was his finest hour. Can you imagine?"

"No," I said. "I guess I'd better keep reading."

The librarian gave me a little salute, and gestured toward one of my favorite tables for reading, or just sitting and thinking. It was true that I couldn't imagine the story she had told me, not really. I could see a pencil with its wood cracked and scratched, the sort you might normally throw away. I could picture an old piano, getting rained on. But I could not imagine the music or the desperation or the menacing ugliness of life in a prison camp. It was a lonely feeling, to think about something I could not imagine. As a writer, my imagination was my most important tool, even more important than a pencil or a scrap of paper. Even before I could write, I could imagine things, but right now my imagination seemed useless, in the face of such truly enormous suffering.

My friend the shoemaker lived for awhile in such a place, a prison camp full of starvation and death. She did not choose to live there, of course. She was imprisoned there with her sister, who did not survive. Every morning they would walk together around the grounds of the prison camp, the shoemaker told me, under the watchful eyes of the guards, and here it is necessary to tell you why I call this friend a shoemaker. It was not, for most of her life, what she did for a living. But she was good with her hands and could fashion all kinds of ingenious fixes at the camp, with the meager materials which were around. The guards had noticed this, and asked her to fix their shoes, which had been torn and tattered during the rough winters. Of course, when guards ask something of prisoners, they are not really asking. They are forcing, and the shoemaker was forced to become a shoemaker. For the rest of her life, she sometimes referred to herself as a shoemaker, always with a smile that was sad about her past and grateful it was over.

I cannot imagine it myself, not really, and in a way it seems that the shoemaker and her sister could not really imagine it either, so they imagined something else instead. It is one of the mysteries of the world that you can change the landscape with your mind, that everything around you can move and shift just from the way you are imagining it. The shoemaker told me that as she and her sister walked the grounds of the prison camp, they would pretend it was a fancy country club instead, a place where wealthy people might stroll around talking and eating elegant food. The shoemaker and her sister walked around the prison camp, and talked to each other like people without a care in the world, exchanging tiny complaints about their imaginary country club. "I didn't like the lemon slice they put in my water," the shoemaker would say, in a place where clean water was often impossible to find. "The lettuce in my sandwich was wilted," said her sister, who would soon die of starvation. It is a true story, about where they were and what they imagined, and no matter how often I sit and think about it, I cannot really imagine it.

I sat in the library thinking of it once more, not only the story of the shoemaker, but the story of the composer, both sad and both desperate and in similar, terrible places. Such stories keep happening, again and again and again, and it is one of the world's most upsetting mysteries that this seems never to change. "Few people can be happy," says a famous philosopher, "unless they hate some other person, nation or creed." "Creed" refers to what people believe, and I believe that everyone in the world should feel as welcome and safe as I did in that library. But of course that is not how the story goes. People are unwelcome and unsafe all over the world, and it is other people who make them feel that way. We all do. We are miserable at home, or at school, scared when we walk the streets, and we are terrorized in all sorts of places, ghastly and desperate, all over the globe. Not all suffering is the same, and we are not all suffering at the same time, but every person or nation or creed has had their turn, or is waiting their turn to suffer or to force suffering on us, sometimes so terribly that for some of us, at some moment somewhere in the world, the only escape is into the world of the imagination, because we cannot really imagine what is happening and what we have done. We have poisoned ourselves, I thought, looking at the scrap of paper in my hand, and felt so overwhelmed, so bewildered there in the library, that I looked around the room for the librarian again, so I could ask her once more what to do.

Except I knew her answer, of course: keep reading, and I took the small book out of my pocket, the one I had been reading at breakfast. It was an old book of poetry, much older than the work of Emily Dickinson who was busying herself with something at her desk. I thought it might be of some comfort, in my bewilderment, to read a few lines from this book, which I had read several times before. I had marked my favorite poems in the table of contents, and made a few notes, here and there, in the margins.

But when I opened the book I found no comfort, and certainly no cure for my bewildered state. If anything I was more bewildered. For I saw, in the margins, the notes I had made. My handwriting has often been described, by various adults who believed it was their job to improve me, as "unclear," and it is true it drifts here and there, into its own shapes and loops, as if the letters are wandering around town, instead of marching in a straight line. But my handwriting is always clear to me, and it was clear to me at that moment. I knew that it was my own handwriting, not only in the margins of the book, but on the scrap of paper that had bewildered me all day.

Chapter Twelve

You had poison for breakfast.
      This is how I write. I think of the finished book, such as the one you are now holding in your hands, as a little animal, doing its specific animal tasks: making little noises, pecking at something on the ground, and interacting with other animals in the barnyard of literature. It is a chicken, in other words, and the egg it sprang from is the finished manuscript, a phrase which here means "neatly typed up pages with all of the sentences looked over carefully for grammatical

mistakes or spelling errers." That egg, my final manuscript, comes from an earlier draft of the book, which is typed up and then covered in scratched-out phrases and added paragraphs and big curvy arrows moving parts of the book from one place to the other, my pen clucking and squawking all over this chicken of a draft. There are several more drafts before this one, like another egg and another chicken and so on and so forth, as I decide what to put into the story, and what to leave out, which is why this finished book contains the book about David and the film about Eve but not the book about Leander and the film about Lady Sylvia, even though I like those too.

Before these previous drafts of this book are various ideas for what the book might be. I write down these ideas in a notebook I keep with me, but not always. I have instructed myself, over and over, to keep my notebook handy at all times, but if you told me to describe myself in one word, it would be "not very good at following directions." Sometimes my notebook is in my other coat, or in the pocket of a different pair of pants from the one I am wearing. Sometimes I have left it in another room, or in a different office, or even once in the back of a taxicab I had managed to track down on a rainy day. Sometimes it is on the shore, and I am miles away in the open water, but sometimes it is nearby and I am simply too lazy to stand up or reach down or stretch over or look under to find it, but often the idea is so exciting that I cannot wait, and when that happens I write down my idea on anything I can find, on index cards or graph paper, old shopping lists or bookmarks, and of course on scraps of paper, small and white like eggshells, that flutter in the breeze like the feathers of chickens. They trail behind me wherever I go, and I find them everywhere, on desks and in drawers and left on bookshelves and fallen on the floor, where I had found one this morning that told me I had poison for breakfast.

It might seem unbelievable to you that I did not recognize my own scrap of paper, or my own handwriting, or the idea I'd had myself. But I believed it. There are so many objects that I find that I have forgotten about until they are in my hands again, and they remind me of times in my life I had otherwise forgotten, the way you will visit a place you think is new and then something, a sound or smell or some tiny detail, will make you realize it is familiar after all. It is even like that with books. I have not forgotten any of my books, but sometimes when I open one up—*Shouldn't You Be In School?* for example, or *29 Myths on the Swinster Pharmacy*—I cannot believe that it is my own work, that it came from a finished manuscript which came from a draft which came from another draft which came from an idea on a scrap of paper which came from my hand, and now here it is, a finished book, coming home to roost in the mind of whoever might read it.

I looked around the room, which was empty except for the scrap of paper I was holding, and the book I was reading, and the table and chair I was using, and the other chairs and tables and the other patron in the library and shelf after shelf of literature and Emily Dickinson, smiling at me, and I told myself that this was a silly way to describe a room, to say it was empty except for many, many things. In the next draft the sentence should be better, I thought, and shorter too. Almost always, shortening a sentence improves it. A nice short sentence feels like something has been left out, which helps give it the element of surprise.

You had poison for breakfast.

I had spent all day investigating this sentence, because, as I explained to the librarian, I preferred not to die. But that was a ridiculous thing to say. I knew I would die. I had just been thinking about it that morning, that we are all going to die. The end of your life is like the open manhole you'll fall into one day while walking around, that one terrible step which will leave you in thin air and then darkness and then nothing.

"Bye bye doggie," the figure of Death will say, and you'll vanish from the world, as grocers and goatherds and shoemakers have done before you, and as time passes the duration of your life keeps getting shorter. Each meal you eat is poison, because the food is just moving you through the world and the end of your time in it. Dinner is poison, and lunch. Brunch and eleveneses and both afternoon and bedtime snacks are poison, and so is breakfast the next morning, all these meals bringing us closer and closer to death. This had occurred to me and I had written it down, and I am writing it down now.

It was a bewildering thought, but the history of literature is the history of bewilderment. Writers all over the world and all across history have been bewildered by the world and all the things in it they cannot imagine, which is why they are—*we* are—writing them down, to try and imagine them.

The poem I had been reading, for instance, when I spotted my own handwriting in the margins, goes like this:

Neither war, nor cyclones, nor earthquakes
Are as terrifying as this oaf,
who stares, sips water, and remembers
Everything we say.

That is the whole poem, written a long time ago in one language and translated more recently into another one. I do not understand it at all. "Oaf" is a word for someone clumsy and ridiculous, but I do not understand how or why a clumsy and ridiculous person could remember everything we say. I do not understand why this oaf is sipping water, or why that is worse than war or cyclones or earthquakes, which are disasters involving people, wind and the earth moving around. I like this poem but I do not understand it, and I suspected that the author and translator, when they wrote and translated it in different continents and thousands of years apart, were just as bewildered as I was when I read it. This is what gave me the idea, the philosophy of this book.

Nobody knows anything at all. We have no idea what is happening. We are all bewildered. Someone may say that they understand something, to ourselves or to others, but they are wrong, or guessing, or making it up. I don't know why I used to sneak out at night and run down the street, and neither do you. I don't know why an eccentric woman cursed the Emerson family whose daughter Sally married Stephen Jones, as her parents had hoped, and neither do any of your friends. Your father, if you have one, cannot unravel Zeno's paradoxes, and your mother, if you can find her, does not know why some shops have daringly erratic hours. Not a single teacher of yours can explain if F. W. Bain really translated his books from old Sanskrit manuscripts or why he pretended to do so, or what Korla Pandit, *née* John Redd, was trying to say in the universal language of music, and if you ask them they will probably not even understand these very simple questions. None of your friends knows why I like swimming in open water or if there is a God, and if you ask them they will probably just shrug at these very complicated questions. Your cousins don't know what the man did wrong, in the song sung by the woman with the adventurous and challenging life, and the person closest to you at this very moment, right over there, cannot explain why the loneliest people in the whole wide world are the ones you're never going to see again. Not a single person understands kissing. No one knows why I am clumsy. I don't know why cactuses are poisonous or why so many people have been forced into prison camps and other terrible situations. I can't even figure out what's wrong with people who don't like poached eggs. I recently made one for a young man, so young some people call him a boy. He had never had a poached egg and had no interest in trying one. I tried to encourage him by saying it was fluffy and it wouldn't kill him. He disagreed, and pointed out that even if it were fluffy, that it would still kill him, because eventually he would die, and I don't know why his reply gave me an idea.

Nevertheless, he tried his best to eat the egg. We must try, all of us, a lot of the time, our best, and we must keep trying. We do not understand anything but we should try our best to understand each other. We should swim and walk in parks, thinking. We should watch movies and think about what might happen. We should buy food and think about where it comes from, and we should listen to music and wonder what it means. We should have conversations, real and imaginary, with translators handy so that everybody might understand everything we say. We may feel native to where we are, or feel displaced, or both, the way someone going on a journey is also a stranger in town, but nevertheless we should keep reading. We must read mysterious literature, and be as bewildered by it as we are by the world, and we should write down our ideas, turning our stories, as if by magic, into literature.

Many years ago, I was crying very hard on a bench outside. I was crying because there was someone I would never really see again. A man happened by whom I knew—not a friend, not even an associate. Truthfully, I had always thought he was something of an oaf. He was all dressed up in a fancy suit, and he was in a hurry. It is very embarrassing to cry when other people can see you, but it is something we all do eventually. The man saw me, and I saw him see me. I did not know where he was going, and he did not know why I was crying. He did not keep hurrying, which would have embarrassed me, and he did not give me a big hug and tell me everything was going to be all right, which would have made me cry harder. He stopped and sat next to me and did not speak a word. He did not say anything at all, and I could not tell you why it was the most perfect thing to do. It was a terrible time for me, but it was, perhaps, his finest hour.

I had not thought of that story in a while, and I was glad to do so. When I was done thinking about it, I closed my book, and nodded goodbye to the librarian. I put the scrap of paper in my pocket, and I never saw it again. It is an old story—*somebody loses something*. Perhaps it fell out of my pocket and into the hands of another reader, who was frightened and inspired to go on a journey, or perhaps it just withered away in my pocket. In any case, I no longer needed it. Its message had been received and understood, and it was time for me to get to work. I couldn't wait. I left the library and tried to get my thoughts in order.

Chapter Thirteen

1. Here you are, Snicket.
2. You have an idea for a book you will write.
3. It is a mystery.
4. It is a book of philosophy.
5. It is about bewilderment.
6. It will be called *Poison for Breakfast*.
7. Remember to include the element of surprise.
8. Remember to leave out certain things.
9.

10. Yes, nobody knows the other rule.
11. It's bewildering.
12. Nevertheless, keep trying your best.
13. First, though, you're hungry. What will you have for lunch?

NOTES

As I've said, everything in this book is true, although some people and places have been given different names so they will not be embarrassed and/or trespassed on. If you are interested in learning more about the things mentioned in this book, these notes might be helpful to you. Some of the things are considered inappropriate for children, so if you are a child, you might ask an adult before finding them, or at least not get caught finding them for yourself.

Chapter One

The poem calling the sea "a case of knives" is "Wading at Wellfleet," by Elizabeth Bishop, who wrote many excellent poems.

The author I said I would not identify is Sophie Blackall.

"The Highwayman" is one of the few good poems by Alfred Noyes.

Chapter Two

The book concerning funerals in ancient Egypt is *The Egyptian Book of the Dead*. My copy is translated by Ramses Saleem. The authors are unknown.

The story about the Emerson family and the eccentric woman and Stephen Jones is called "Witch's Revenge" and is from a book called *Strangely Enough*, by C. B. Colby.

The writer who taught me that "A Stranger Comes to Town" and "Someone Goes on a Journey" are the same thing is Ellen Miller, the author of a single book, *Like Being Killed*.

I should also acknowledge the writer Vladimir Nabokov, in whose novel *Lolita* is the parenthetical phrase "(picnic, lightning)" to explain someone's death. I admire this phrase and use many similar phrases in this chapter. *Lolita* is a book some people think is particularly dangerous to young people, and so I will not recommend it, but merely mention it is one of the most fantastic novels in the world, and leave it at that.

Chapter Three

The wonderful book my neighbor was reading is *The Headless Cupid*, by Zilpha Keatley Snyder.

The paradox by Zeno is called Achilles and the Tortoise. Zeno thought up several other paradoxes, most of which are interesting. There are many books on Zeno and his paradoxes, both good and bad.

Chapter Four

The movie I saw when I was young is called *Midnight*. It is directed by Mitchell Leisen and written by Charles Brackett and Billy Wilder, from a story by Edwin Justus Mayer and Franz Schulz.

Chapter Five

A Syrup of the Bees by F. W. Bain is a real book.

Korla Pandit is a real musician.

Everything You Know about Indians Is Wrong is by Paul Chaat Smith.

Ceylon is currently called Sri Lanka.

Chapter Six

Little Red Riding Hood is the hero of a story which is usually named after her. There are many versions, some good and some bad.

Oedipus is the hero of *Oedipus Rex*, by Sophocles.

The Japanese story about the feudal lord is described in a book called *The Izu Dancer and Other Stories*. The book has two authors and two translators, but the section in question is written by Yaushi Inoue and translated by Leon Picon.

A rabbi named Julie Saxe-Taller helped me understand tzimtzum, as much as anyone can understand such a thing. I recommend learning from a rabbi to everyone, even rabbis.

The writer who said, "God made everything out of nothing, but the nothingness shows through" is Paul Valéry, from his book about bad thoughts.

The book I lost and then found again is *The Story of Junk* by Linda Yablonsky.

Chapter Seven

The song in the supermarket is "Sinnerman," as performed by Nina Simone.

Persia is now often called Iran.

Chapter Eight

"300 Goats" is by Naomi Shahib Nye.

The song suggesting that the loneliest people in the whole wide world are the ones you're never going to see again is "Harlem Roulette," written by John Darnielle and first performed by his band the Mountain Goats.

Chapter Nine

The author and translator with whom I had the imaginary conversation are Pu Songling and John Minford, respectively. The book in question is *Strange Tales from a Chinese Studio*.

Chapter Ten

The composer who does not move the notes around is Morton Feldman. My favorite of his pieces is probably "Crippled Symmetry."

The book with the girl and the cave and the tiger is *The Long Secret* by Louise Fitzhugh, often described, inaccurately, as a sequel to *Harriet the Spy*.

Chapter Eleven

Emily Dickinson is a real poet. None of her poems had titles, so they were numbered, although sometimes the numbers get mixed up. My favorite begins "I tie my Hat" and is usually numbered 443.

The composer in the prison camp is Olivier Messiaen, and the piece he composed there is *Quartet for the End of Time*. It is my librarian's favorite Messiaen piece, but mine is *Fête des belles eaux*.

The philosopher who said that few people can be happy without hating some other person, etc., is Bertrand Russell.

Chapter Twelve

The poem about the oaf is by Antipatros of Thessalonika, and was written in ancient Greek. It was translated into English by Kenneth Rexroth, who is a poet himself.

It seems important to note that almost all of this book was written in a public library, and I would like to thank the staff and patrons of the library for being so quiet and helpful, except for one patron who was quite nasty to me.

Chapter Thirteen

There is no note for Chapter Thirteen.